When Your Heart Belongs to an Addict

When Your Heart Belongs to an Addict

A Healing Perspective

by Cyndee Rae Lutz

FLIP THE HIPPO PUBLISHING
Centennial, CO

Library of Congress Catalog Number: 2016912964
ISBN: 978-0-9978564-0-8 print
ISBN: 978-0-9978564-1-5 e-book

Publisher's Cataloging-In-Publication Data
(Prepared by The Donohue Group, Inc.)

Names: Lutz, Cyndee Rae.
Title: When your heart belongs to an addict : a healing perspective /
    [Cyndee Rae Lutz].
Description: [First edition]. | Centennial, CO : Flip the Hippo Publishing,
    [2016] | Includes bibliographical references.
Identifiers: ISBN 978-0-9978564-0-8 (print) |
    ISBN 978-0-9978564-1-5 (ebook)
Subjects: LCSH: Lutz, Cyndee Rae. | Parents of drug addicts--Psychology. |
    Drug addicts--Family relationships. | Spirituality. | Codependency. |
    Mind and body.
Classification: LCC HV5824.Y68 L88 2016 (print) | LCC HV5824.Y68 (ebook) |
    DDC 362.290835--dc23

Editor: Joan Sherman
Designer: Kimberlee Lynch
Proofreader: Jenna Browning

Printed in the USA

Flip the Hippo Publishing
Centennial, CO

www.cyndeeraelutz.com

To all those who suffer with addiction
and those who love them.
May you come to the sure knowledge
that your life matters and find peace at last.

Contents

Preface

I cannot promise that the addict or alcoholic in your life will make it—no one can give such a guarantee. Some addicts and alcoholics will die. Some will do time in prison. Some will live with their disease for many, many years. And others, even those who seem to be the worst off, will get well.

What I can tell you is that you are far more powerful and worthwhile than your loved one's addiction would lead you to believe.

In the beginning, you may not think your loved one is addicted. You know that something isn't right and that things aren't going as planned, but addiction may not enter your mind. Even as clues start to arise and accumulate, you still may question whether you are imagining things—or making things out to be worse than they are. You might seek information or connect with certain people in hopes of coming across answers to the core questions that have been tormenting you: "Is my loved one an addict/alcoholic?" and "Is it really a problem?" The answer I like best for the latter question is simply this: "It's a problem if his or her drinking or drugging affects your life negatively."

Like me, you may never have dealt with addiction before. You may be unfamiliar with the patterns, mannerisms, or characteristics of addiction. Once you gather more information, you might still question whether or not your loved one is truly addicted. After all, this couldn't happen to *your* child, spouse, relative, or friend, right? They're bright and talented, you reason, and they had a good upbringing, had tons of friends, and were active in sports, the community, or other endeavors.

What I can tell you is that you are far more powerful and worthwhile than your loved one's addiction would lead you to believe.

Addiction takes many forms: drugs, alcohol, gambling, food, pornography, and the list goes on. In this book, I mainly address substance abuse, but the strategies in these pages can improve the lives of anybody whose loved one faces addiction. To help you determine whether your loved one is addicted to drugs or alcohol, consider the following list of common characteristics observed in addicts:

Lying
Manipulation
Stealing
Financial Problems
Legal Issues
Inability to Hold a Job
Weight Loss
Isolation
Lack of Care about Personal Appearance
Personality Changes
Irritability
Relationship Issues
Increased Illness
Blaming Others or Situations for Their Problems

None of us sets out to become the loved one of an addict, just as our loved one didn't plan to become addicted. I *never* imagined that I would be the mother of an addicted child. In fact, I vehemently resisted the notion for months. I had a very long pity party for myself before I finally accepted the reality I was facing. I felt cheated. I did *not* want to be the mother of an addict. That was simply not what I had envisioned for my life—or for my son. I didn't want to deal with it. I didn't know *how* to deal with it. I kept thinking that something would miraculously change and he would get better. Things would go back to the way they were, and we could continue merrily on our way to the bright future I had always dreamed of for my family.

It took me an awfully long time to learn that I didn't have to be defined by the role I'd been thrust into—mother of an addict—but I did need to accept the reality of the situation at hand in order to deal with it. My son was addicted to drugs. All my best-laid plans and all the love in the world weren't helping to save him. His life and my own were spiraling out of control. Something had to change. I didn't know it right away, but that something would be me.

In the thirteen-plus years since my education surrounding addiction began, I've learned many things. I've become an expert on a topic that I never wanted to know anything about. I understand what it feels like to be held hostage emotionally, to be worn down by my son's belittling words, manipulative and dishonest tendencies, and blatant disregard for his own welfare or for those he once cared about. I've experienced the shame and isolation that accompanied his erratic and senseless behavior. I have lived in daily fear, terrified that my son would die, harm someone else, or end up in prison, and I have felt the overwhelming sadness at the loss of the amazing person he once was, before addiction swallowed us both whole. Any brief moments of personal happiness or peace depended entirely on his current mood and state of being.

In truth, I have learned a great deal more than I ever cared to about addiction. But the wealth of information I've acquired has helped me deal with this heart-wrenching affliction and shown me how to bring some measure of peace, normalcy, and even joy to my life once again.

I've combined my experiences as an entrepreneur, businesswoman, yoga teacher, Al-Anon sponsor (working with the loved ones of alcoholics), and mentor to weave together many different and powerful ideas and philosophies. The information I've gathered is both spiritual and practical in nature.

If you believed in God before you confronted the addiction problem in your life, you may now feel that same God has let you down terrifically. Therefore, this book includes different perspectives that give you an opportunity to redefine and enhance your connection to a Higher Guidance, whether in the context of a defined religion or not.

The practical tools included in the book allow you to recognize behaviors and characteristics common in those who love an addict, as well as anyone who has felt at the mercy of a dysfunctional, dependent relationship. I provide options that allow you to react and behave differently in situations with your loved one, and I explain how to create and establish boundaries that protect your own well-being at the same time.

Understanding how you've unknowingly disempowered yourself in the process of trying to help your loved one is imperative if you want to change the status quo that has been causing you so much heartache and misery. You might've been thinking that your addict is the one with the problem, but if you are honest, you will admit that elements of your own life have become unmanageable as well. Your loved one is addicted to drugs or alcohol, and you've become addicted to fixing him or her. Your failed attempts have left you weary, with your own worth in question.

But remember this: *your well-being is paramount!* It is crucial that you don't lose yourself in your loved one's battle with addiction. This book will help you reclaim the many precious aspects of your life that have been totally forgotten, ignored, or set aside while you've been trying to save your addict. The tools will be useful whether or not the addict is currently using. Reclaiming your life is an absolutely essential step for your renewal and for your own mental and physical health. And it just might be the most important thing that you can do for your loved one: often, when you get better, they get better too!

Acknowledgments

Joan Sherman, my developmental editor, for helping to direct and refine the book's message and for being a great cheerleader throughout the entire process.

One of my dearest friends and the most creative person I know, Kimberlee Lynch, who designed my logo, the book's cover, and its layout. Thank you for always supporting and understanding my creative nature. You are my portal for all things wacky and mind-blowing.

My sons. You are my two greatest creations. You have allowed me to see the world through a mother's eyes and experience the greatest and most fierce love on Earth.

Hansa Knox, owner of Prana Yoga and Ayurveda Mandala in Denver, who made it possible for me to begin yoga teacher training and for telling me that it didn't matter if I ever did a headstand.

My sweet husband, Jon, who by proximity experiences the highs and lows that accompany my endeavors. Your calm presence and unwavering strength of character support me and encourage me to dance in my own light.

My faithful furry companions, Sophie and Theo, who are always nearby when I work, and let me know when it's time to take a break.

To my Higher Guidance, which supported me when I stepped out in faith.

1

Pain: The Price of Admission for Change

The Damn Sad Truth—My Story

"Given your son's history of opiate abuse, I think he should start a methadone program. His chances of recovery are 10 percent." My son was only eighteen at the time I heard those words, but his life and mine would be forever changed. As much as I wanted to believe what the doctor said wasn't true, I had heard the words correctly—and they have been indelibly etched in my mind ever since.

The fear and finality of those words from the doctor at the detoxification center struck me hard in the gut and broke my heart at the same time. Never before had I truly realized the seriousness of what we faced. I tried to be strong for my son. I could tell he, too, was taken aback by the news.

One of the saddest things in the world is to watch an amazing, vibrant, and talented person lose himself needlessly by numbing out and denying his worth, especially when that person is your child. As time would show, I would lose myself in the battle for his well-being, fighting against a demon far stronger than I could comprehend. What began as deep fear for him turned into a deep fear of everything, ultimately requiring me to abandon the person I had thought I was until then.

Neither one of us would ever be the same.

Crushed by Fear

Over the next few weeks, as I came to understand just how dire my son's situation was, it seemed to me that the world slipped off its axis. So much in my life, in my mind, in my attitudes, and even in my imagination changed. Things I had taken for granted suddenly felt precarious and fragile, my own self-confidence eroded, and all that once was solid and predictable and real in my world seemed to have been swept away, replaced by uncertainty, self-doubt, and fear.

• I wondered whether the clothes I put on in the morning would be appropriate when I got the call telling me that my child was dead. After all, I might need to go to the hospital or the morgue, possibly talk with detectives, police, or other authorities. It could be a long and exhausting day, lasting well into the night. No heels. I'd need really comfortable shoes and clothing that wouldn't interfere with the tasks at hand.

• I learned to hide cash and valuables after having cameras, stereo equipment, tools, jewelry, and cash stolen from my house and pawned for drugs on multiple occasions. I was always afraid that I'd forgotten to hide something when my son came to visit. And I was ashamed that I had to resort to such measures because I didn't trust him.

- I felt anxious when my phone rang. The sound put me into an immediate panic; it was the same with the doorbell and the mail delivery. They all seemed to bring incessant bad news—from rehab personnel, police, my son's probation officer, his school, his disbelieving father, or an unhappy neighbor.

- My mind was constantly preoccupied, racing and reacting to imaginary, worst-case scenarios as well as concrete and virtually daily troubles, all at the same time. I was afraid I might not be able to function at my job and worried about my mental health. I began taking an antidepressant to help me cope with the anxiety. I had no idea how to deal with it at the time.

I was catapulted into a constant state of panic, always waiting for the next piece of bad news. It felt like everything that happened was negative and only getting worse. My life became unmanageable. Dread followed me everywhere; it permeated every cell of my being and shadowed every move I made.

The Early Years and the Decade from Hell

It wasn't always like this. There was a time when some would say I lived a charmed life. I grew up with parents, grandparents, and other close family members who all loved me. I was never beaten, verbally abused, or sexually molested. We didn't have much money, but I never went cold or hungry. I was forty-one years old before the first person I loved died.

Looking back, I can see that the chaos started when my marriage to my sons' father ended. The divorce came when the boys were twelve and fourteen. I now realize that the fear of change—for all of us, especially for my children—had kept me in the marriage much longer than I would've imagined. I hadn't felt safe or strong enough to make any changes for years. As a stay-at-home mom, I depended financially on my husband. I had been with him for twenty years, and married for seventeen. I was thirty-eight years old when we split.

I could have handled the situation far better than I did—if I knew then what I know now. But I didn't. I wish I'd had a greater sense of my own worth and of my right to express my individuality. But I didn't. I wish more than just about anything that my kids didn't have to suffer like they did, that I could've protected them more from the damaging effects of a very messy divorce. But I couldn't. I deeply regret that.

While the divorce was in progress, I began working full-time in the financial industry. After three years, I left to start a magazine to help others harmed by divorce, *Divorce in Denver—Moving Forward*. During this period, both of my sons began experimenting with marijuana and alcohol.

Life was really, really hard during those years, filled with constant uncertainty. Coparenting was difficult and ever-changing, and I missed my boys so much when they were with their father. Both my jobs as a financial sales representative and as a magazine publisher completely depended on the business I brought in, which added a great deal of pressure to the mix. I had no clue things could get even harder, but they did.

I sold the magazine after three years and went back to work in the financial industry. When my youngest son was about sixteen years old, his drug use progressed to include prescription opiates, and that ultimately led to heroin. (This is where people typically gasp, for the word *heroin* conjures up terrible images for most of us. The terrible truth is that modern-day abusers of opiates are highly likely to make the switch to heroin because it is a much cheaper way to get a similar high.)

I don't think my son or his friends understood what they were getting themselves into when they began raiding medicine cabinets. They thought the drugs were safer because they had been prescribed. Many of those friends are now dead or still suffering.

Before heading to college, my older son also had his share of trouble but nothing quite as severe as my younger son experienced—and things were about to come to a head with him.

By age seventeen, he began spinning out of control. Thefts, lies, cops, and strange people became common elements in his life. He dropped out of high school in his senior year and would see the inside of a jail cell on a couple of occasions.

The crisis peaked when middle-of-the-night calls to his father and to me began increasing and his behavior became more erratic than ever. He sneaked out of his dad's home one night, stole his car, and ended up in a terrible neighborhood in Denver trying to buy drugs. The cops who phoned his dad after they picked our son up said the vehicle had been carjacked. His dad decided to press charges against our son because we thought he would be safer in jail than anywhere else given the state he was in. When he was released the following day, we took him to a detox center, and I arranged for him to go to a rehab facility afterward. I had given my notice at work the week before. My job ended the following Friday, and on Monday, I flew with my son to his drug rehabilitation center. It would be the first of many.

Just When Things Started Looking Better

About five months later and after a different rehab for our son, my ex-husband died of a heart attack at age fifty. It came as a total shock. None of us could believe that he was actually gone.

We all flew to Nebraska, his birthplace, for the funeral. In our own way, we each tried to wrap our arms around the magnitude of what his death would mean for us. My newly sober younger son relapsed at the funeral, and my older son began getting into a lot of trouble when he returned to college (drinking, fighting, fraternity pranks) and almost got kicked out. I felt badly that my sons had to deal with such a tragic loss in their young lives, but at the same time, I found myself feeling very angry. I was bitter that my former husband had left behind an even bigger mess for me to clean up by myself.

At that point, adrift and anguished, I began a ten-month yoga teacher training course. I didn't really intend to teach yoga, but I knew I needed to do *something* that would bring a measure of sanity and peace to my life. I thought yoga might help me. Fortunately, the teacher understood my precarious situation. I told her I didn't know whether I could follow through with the ten-month commitment, but she accepted me into the program nonetheless and told me that if things got too hard, I could drop out and she wouldn't charge me for the missed time. I proceeded because I really had nowhere else to turn and nothing left to lose.

In those early days, I couldn't comprehend how one could ever find joy in life again amid the uncertainty, worry, and fear that were my constant companions. In the past, I had always been able to devise creative solutions to problems I encountered, but now, as much as I tried, I could not find an answer for my youngest son, who was once again mired in his addiction. Early on, a counselor had told me that the average number of relapses for an addict is eight. I was astonished—both frightened and yet comforted by that statement (maybe my son's situation wasn't impossible after all,

I reasoned). I can't swear that statistic is accurate, but I have learned that relapsing is indeed very common. My son's relapse was all too typical.

Around that time, I began attending Al-Anon meetings for the loved ones of addicts and alcoholics, which I highly recommend to anyone. I chose to go to Al-Anon instead of Nar-Anon—for the loved ones of those who abuse drugs—simply because I like the group, and ultimately they're dealing with the same issue. Initially, I had thought that I was healthy and that my son was the one with the problem. I would soon learn how wrong I was. The truth is that his addiction had robbed the spirit from both of us—and I was as sick as he was.

I continued the yoga training and ended up not only loving yoga but teaching it as well. I consider Al-Anon and yoga to be two of the greatest gifts I've received in my lifetime, but I might never have found either one if it weren't for my desperate need to try something different and find a new approach to our problems.

Looking back, I realize I would certainly *never* choose to go through the painful events we experienced. Yet I've since learned that what I thought might kill my youngest son—and take me down as well—has also been a cleverly disguised gift.

The Gift of Desperation and the Virtue of Brazen Openness

We all have our hearts broken and our dreams crushed at some point, maybe numerous times in our lives. In reality, most of us are just a phone call away from having our world fall apart. My goal and passion is to extend some of the insight I've gleaned from my own heartaches and experiences—to show others how they can face and deal with adversity or their worst fears and by doing so transform life into a most extraordinary experience.

Contrary to what I imagined in the darkest hours with my son, I have found that our lives are not a perpetual tragedy as we wait for release upon our demise. Instead, I now know that we can use our pain as fuel to launch us into another dimension. It worked for me, and I would be remiss not to share that knowledge with others.

I had tried everything imaginable to control the unmanageable situations erupting in my life, and the extraordinary effort left me exhausted and numb. I couldn't hide my pain and despair, and I was stripped of all my masks, left with only shattered pieces of who I once was (or who I had thought I was).

With no other choice, I began the search for something more. I became willing to try a new approach, *anything* that might ease the pain. Brazen openness is the key to change: a willingness to see things differently, letting go of any preconceived notions of what defined us previously. Feeling weak and exposed isn't fun, but it's a great place to be if you need to invite change. Fortunately (or unfortunately), suffering through pain, heartache, and deep despair is often the price we must pay for creating change. We rarely change because we want to; we change because we *have* to. Life becomes so unbearable that we are forced into transformation—all the while kicking, screaming, and desperately clinging to familiar feelings and responses. We do not realize there is any other way until we finally let go and open up to whatever opportunities may arise. Practicing brazen openness can be incredibly uncomfortable and scary, but it is definitely worth the effort.

We learn that we can't change the people around us or the things that happen as a result of their behavior. Instead, we come to understand that we ourselves have to get better if our loved ones are to stand a chance of improving. In fact, not only do we need to get better; we have a right to that opportunity and an obligation to seize it. We each have a responsibility to live our own lives, as only we can.

Every one of the tools I'll share in the pages ahead have proven powerful in my own transformation. I have watched and helped others change their lives as well. I know these tools work, whether you're dealing with a major crisis or you're hoping to change direction in life. I've adopted and intermingled many traditions and philosophies in the work I've done as a yoga teacher, as a sponsor in Al-Anon, as an entrepreneur and business consultant, and as an everyday nurturer for those who wish to find new meaning in their lives. Undoubtedly, you will find something here that piques your curiosity and can be implemented in your life. Take what resonates with you and leave the rest behind.

Brazen openness is the key to change:
a willingness to see things differently,
letting go of any preconceived notions of
what defined us previously.

2

Loving an Alcoholic
or Drug Addict Can
Take You Down …
Period

The Distorted Thinking That Arises

When you love someone who is dealing with addiction or alcoholism, you often don't realize the blow it delivers to your own self-esteem. Addicts and alcoholics don't always like to suffer alone. They'll take those who are closest to them right down with them.

Many of us develop certain coping mechanisms in our attempt to deal with their altered states of mind and erratic behaviors. In the process, our own thinking often becomes distorted and abnormal. Here are some examples of the distorted thinking that arises in such situations:

• **Distorted sense of power and the need to control.** You want them to change. You take it upon yourself to provide solutions and information in order to convince them that there's a better way. It becomes one of your daily jobs. You think you know best and have all the right answers and say to yourself, "If only they would listen to me, then everything would be okay." When they don't heed your advice, you might spend outrageous amounts of time formulating solutions for some of the most unbelievable situations you imagine or find yourselves in. Then you second-guess everything you do anyway, unsure if your approach will work or have the effect you intend. You don't have time to invest in anything else, anyone else, or even yourself as you try to control shaky situations and prevent everything in your world from falling apart.

• **Distorted sense of blame, shame, and responsibility.** You vacillate between blaming them and feeling responsible for what they are going through. You fear that you are failing in your responsibility to them. Perhaps it's something you did or didn't do that made them drink or turn to drugs. If only you had been smarter in your decisionmaking; if only you had been a better parent, friend, or spouse. In the next moment, you may feel smug and superior to them because, after all, you aren't the one with the problem. You treat your addict like a child, as though they are inferior, looking down on them and blaming them for the current circumstances. Over time, though, you become resentful and develop a deep-seated grudge against them. Paradoxically, though, you love them dearly and can't conceive of living without them. Meanwhile, you are caught in a confusing mishmash of emotions.

• **Distorted perspective regarding the future/projecting bad outcomes.** You are always expecting the worst to happen or waiting for the other shoe to drop. There are times, especially during the height of addiction and alcoholism, when everything seems to go terribly wrong; you can't imagine an end to it—or a good ending, anyway. Many of you have dealt with situations such as a kid dropping out of school, a spouse missing work, a loved one landing in jail or in the hospital, a child living on the streets, car wrecks, illicit affairs, and suicide attempts or overdoses. So you know bad things do happen. You live in fear of these outcomes nearly every day—and during crises, almost every minute you're awake.

• **Distorted sense of worth.** You feel beaten down by their addiction and become silent, numb, and resigned. You lose your voice in the world and at home. Once upon a time, you were afraid for them. Then you also become afraid of them. Addicts are master manipulators and can be both verbally and physically abusive. You often take the brunt of their anger, pain, and unease. Your self-esteem is shot, and you don't know how to stand up for yourself. In fact, you don't even have the energy to try. When you do occasionally gather the courage to speak up, they somehow twist everything you say and end up making it sound like you are the one who is wrong—or possibly crazy. You might even start believing it yourself.

Your thinking continues to be distorted as you mistakenly correlate their addictive tendencies with your own self-worth. As their disease progresses and if you lack help from others who've been in a similar situation, you may eventually take on the following characteristics:

• **You become a doormat.** Unsure of how to change things or set boundaries, you overlook, excuse, and allow damaging behaviors. Maybe you've been in the situation so long that you don't know how to distinguish acceptable behavior from unacceptable behavior. Your gauge of normalcy is broken, and you're confused about what is unreasonable and improper; dealing with the "small stuff" seems unnecessary and futile while you conserve your energy to handle the "big stuff." Another reason you enable poor behavior is the fear that you aren't "standing by" them when they need you. You don't want that burden on your shoulders. You love them so much and would never want them to feel the same way you do—alone, lost, and afraid.

• **You isolate yourself.** You create a facade to present to the outside world so no one knows what is really happening. You disable your personal support system. You're afraid to let anyone know about the crazy world in which you live. Or you might discuss your personal situation with people who have no experience in the matter and find they just don't understand. You don't want others to judge you or your addict. You're afraid of being in public places or at events with your loved one because they might behave inappropriately and embarrass themselves—and you. Or they might not show up at all. Meanwhile, you don't have the time or energy to take part in hobbies or outings with friends because you have to be available to deal with the next crisis on the home front. As a result, you are left to deal with it all alone. Friends and family members suffer as you devote all your resources to "helping" the addict.

• **Your mental health and well-being suffer.** You spend time worrying about where they are, who they're with, what they're doing. You may snoop on their cell phone or social media, trying to determine what they have been up to so you can either relax (knowing they're okay for now) or prepare for the next catastrophe. It might become common for them to call you in the middle of the night, asking you to come bail them out of jail or some other predicament; therefore, your sleep schedule suffers. They may claim to need money to pay off a drug dealer who will harm them if they don't come through with the cash. Or they may need to have their car insurance paid so they can get to their job, assuming they've been able to hold down a job. It is so hard to know the right thing to do in all of these situations, and you're fearful of the outcomes if you make the wrong call—or fail to act. Trying to juggle your own job on top of all these pressures can overwhelm you. For some, work might be a relief from the day-to-day strain. For others, though, it can be a tremendous challenge, for it's hard to maintain the necessary concentration.

• **You lose control of your own life.** Your existence becomes tightly enmeshed in the addict's. You become codependent. Often, it can take a long time to understand that the addict's or alcoholic's behavior isn't a reflection on you, nor are you responsible for their life turning out well. You become quite interreliant: if they're having a good day, you can have a good day and vice versa. Put another way, your health and happiness hinge on their behavior. You forget what it was like to live "your" life and don't find much that brings you laughter or joy anymore. Many people suffer depression; some even entertain the thought of suicide.

Have You Ever Considered Suicide, Just for a Moment?

·{ MY STORY }·

Some of my life has been so unbearably painful, there have been many times when I have wished my life were over.

One such instance occurred when I called the police on my son, who was about sixteen or seventeen at the time. He had been extremely angry with me that day and exhibited some frightening behaviors. He was arrested briefly and taken to a juvenile detention center.

His dad yelled at me, saying I had done the wrong thing: it was cold in the detention facility, he argued, and our son hadn't been fed. Yet the arresting officer thanked me for being a good parent. Talk about mixed emotions. I hadn't known what else to do at the time to stop my son's damaging behavior. Honestly, I still don't know what I could have done differently.

Seeing him the next day at a hearing, dressed in an orange jumpsuit with his arms and legs shackled, instantly brought me to tears and took my breath away; the memory still breaks my heart into a million pieces. When he was younger, I had thought my son was bright enough to be the president of the United States. He was so capable, smart, and kind. How did we ever wind up in a court proceeding? I certainly had not read about anything like this in my parenting literature.

During one of the required follow-up meetings with authorities, he claimed that I hit him on a regular basis—about once a month. (Great forethought on my part to schedule it so regularly, right?) Being questioned about that almost took me out, consuming the very last shred of self-esteem I had. I could not comprehend how my son could make such a charge, and I wondered how he could lie so flippantly about something so big. I never, ever thought one of my children would intentionally harm me, so this blew my mind. What I didn't know at the time was that *addicts will say anything to take the pressure off themselves.*

In my longing for release from the heartache, I would envision not having to deal with any of it anymore. I would imagine overdosing on pills or driving my car off a cliff. But deep down, I never really thought that I would actually take my own life. I didn't want to die. I just didn't want to feel as badly as I did.

I've since learned that I'm not alone in feeling this way. Many of us who have dealt with traumatic experiences have had such thoughts. Expressing them to a trusted individual with experiences similar to mine helped me to see that I was not the only person dealing with these problems. This friend discerned that I wasn't serious about doing harm to myself; I just needed to reach into the depth of my pain, verbalize it, and briefly entertain the notion of my heartache ending. Having previously been in a similar situation, she didn't have an alarmist reaction to my words. And for me, just knowing that she had been through something like this with her own son, that she had some of the same thoughts I did, and that she was emotionally healthy now helped me feel much less isolated and abnormal.

If you are currently in this place, I encourage you to talk to someone with an experience similar to your own. Al-Anon is a great resource in this regard. However, for something more urgent, seek out a mental health professional or call the National Suicide Prevention Lifeline: 1-800-273-8255. You might want to reference this resource if you know someone else struggling with dark thoughts, such as an addicted acquaintance or another person who loves an addict.

Though I knew deep down that I couldn't take my own life, I *had* hoped for something or someone else to do the job for me. For some strange reason, I wished a bus would hit me. Why a bus, I haven't a clue, and the odds of that happening aren't stellar. Or so I thought.

One morning at about 5:00 a.m., I was out walking near my home, getting my exercise before preparing to head into work. It was very dark. I was beginning to crest a hill when I heard it—the deep rumbling. It sounded like a heavy vehicle with a diesel engine. It got louder and clearly was heading in my direction, but still I couldn't see it. I began to panic and thought to myself, "Is this it? Is this the bus I've envisioned? Is it going to hit me? Am I going to die now?" Then, a more rational thought struck me: "Am I going to let it hit me even though I know it's coming?"

In those few seconds, I grew scared and realized I was afraid to die. I hadn't even thought about dying in a while. Then I began to think how crazy the situation was. As the rumbling reached the top of the hill and as adrenaline still surged through my veins, I finally saw the menacing vehicle: a milk truck making its morning rounds! I laughed aloud, both relieved and a little abashed at my out-of-control imagination.

Fighting for Your Life:
Taking a Different Approach When You've Hit Bottom

At some point, when your pain is too unbearable and you realize your powerlessness to affect the situation you're in, you seek out help. There is no fight left in you anymore. You are weary from trying to cure a problem you didn't create that isn't improving or going away. Gradually, you begin to understand how your own behaviors have complicated your loved one's recovery; you see the ways in which you unintentionally facilitate their abusive tendencies, sabotaging your own well-being in the process. But you are unsure how to change them. It is time to take back control of your life—and give your loved one the dignity to do the same. After all, what you've been doing hasn't worked: in truth, it's likely you find yourself in a worse place than when everything started veering off track.

When you reach this point in a journey that can take months or even years and differs from everyone else's, you are ready to stop fighting solely for your loved one's sobriety and the life you wanted for them and start fighting for your own life as well. *You learn that it is not your responsibility to ensure their life turns out okay,* nor do you have the power to do so, no matter how sincerely you want a good outcome. The bottom line is this: you and your loved one are each responsible for your own happiness. Until you accept this hard fact, you will both stay stuck and miserable.

The flip side is a whole lot brighter: *when you get better, it is very likely that your loved one will too.* When I learned that if I got better it could also help my son, I was on board 100 percent. In retrospect, I'm not sure I really would've done it just for my own benefit because I thought so little of myself at the time, but I would've done *anything* to help *him.* That's when I began changing my perspective and approach toward life. I had to take a hard look at myself to discover the origins of the holes in my self-worth. It has been an invaluable process and one that has made all the difference in my current state of mind, in my relationship with my son and others in my life, and in my perceived value as a human being. It's worth repeating the key point here, as I've witnessed it many times: when we get better, they often get better too.

It is critical that you start the journey to reclaim your life by looking at where and when you first began to give away your power and suppress your own desires. For most people, that initially happened way back when they were young. Some were forced to grow up with addiction and other unhealthy tendencies in the family. Others faced unfortunate life circumstances. And still others just struggled as they tried to navigate their way to the American Dream.

The bottom line is this: you and your loved one are each responsible for your own happiness.

3

Living the Dream— or a Nightmare?

A Life Built on Self-Propulsion

All too often, the American Dream is not what you were led to believe, not all it is cracked up to be. You wake up one day to find that your life isn't working. You look in the mirror and ask yourself, "Is this all there is? Who lied to me?"

Something is missing. What happened to your passion, your dreams, your sense of fulfillment and wonder? Even for those without the additional strain of addiction, happiness can be a fleeting thing. It may come only briefly with the next happy hour, the next break for a latte, or the next episode of your favorite TV program. Meanwhile, you have to juggle a thousand commitments at home and work. You have to shuttle your children to their multiple activities, be attentive to your partner's needs, meet the demands of a demanding boss, and somehow find a way to maintain all those things that capitalism may have provided for you and your family. Then you wake up the next day and do it all over again.

In America, you have so many opportunities to express your uniqueness, yet you are caught up in a life of self-propulsion—perpetuating competitive corporate agendas for career growth, observing political and social protocols, upholding a set of religious rules you may no longer agree with, and subscribing to the dictates of the marketing geniuses who continually push their unrealistic ideas of success down your throat.

You become part of a homogenous mass pursuing every fairy tale ending that promises happiness, pleasure, and the hope of getting ahead. Thus begins the average American's tireless chase to become rich, famous, thin, or whatever else is deemed necessary and popular at the moment.

Molding Yourself in the World's Image: Just Trying to Fit In

Many of you unwittingly hand over your serenity and power to society at large, hoping that your hard work will be recognized and rewarded and that some value will be placed on your very existence as a result. You must "do" something to achieve or validate your worth or merit.

Yet, at best, you find the world is only briefly impressed with your efforts to mold yourself according to society's image. Your value fluctuates, dictated by an ever-changing set of people, rules, and circumstances beyond your control.

We put off the "good stuff" and the "fun people" until we feel we have sacrificed enough and earned the right to enjoy life.

In all your efforts, there is no lasting proof that you matter or make much of a difference. You never quite seem to reach that elusive "plateau of peace" so many long for, the place where striving ceases and life isn't as hard as it once was. You may have thought that if you got the right education, you'd get the right job; if you married the right person, you'd have the perfect family; and if you belonged to the correct religion, God would be on your side. You'd be successful—Easy Street, here I come!

The milestones you once anticipated can be the very ones that leave you feeling stuck, tired, and miserable: a large house, a nice car, and a great job title leave you with a huge mortgage, endless auto payments, and golden handcuffs. Meanwhile, you find there is little time for adequate sleep, for relaxation and creativity, or for being with the people you love and enjoy.

You may admire or identify with celebrities and sports figures, emulating their habits in the way you eat, dress, think, and act. You may compare yourself—no doubt unfavorably—to the superstars of the moment. Can you match the athletic prowess of the latest gridiron hero? Do you have a face or figure like that of the model or actress who graces the cover of every magazine?

Women may even go so far as to have their bodies carved up so that silicone can be inserted underneath their chest muscles, an extremely painful procedure of which I speak from experience: big boobs = better woman. Today, I look back and wonder why anyone in her right mind would do such a thing (with the exception of having breast reconstruction, of course). But that's just it. I wasn't in my right mind when I subjected my body to that surgery. I was coming from a place of fear—fear that I didn't have enough to offer the world and would be judged accordingly.

We put off the "good stuff" and the "fun people" until we feel we have sacrificed enough and earned the right to enjoy life. Over the years, you begin to notice the compromises you have made while trying to live up to unreal ideals—time and youth forever gone, meaningful careers never explored, enjoyable hobbies now abandoned, relationships withered away, and unhealthy lifestyles all too easily adopted. Meanwhile, some of the people you love dearly suffer and die, and you're left with the pain and emptiness caused by their loss and by the loss of your own dreams.

It's Never Enough—The Futile Pursuit of Things

No matter how many material goods and modern conveniences you accumulate as you chase the American Dream, they will never be enough because none of them can take away the suffering intrinsic to the human experience.

I can assure you that driving in a slick red sports car wouldn't have eased the pain of taking my son to rehab, any more than going home to a beautiful house would have removed the ache in my heart from watching him suffer at his own hands.

In typical American fashion, we don't want to deal with death or dying or the bad things that happen to all of us. We'd rather cover them up, shove them aside, and ignore the ugly aspects of life. We want to act as though the ugliness doesn't exist—at least for us, anyway—because we are handling our lives just fine, thank you very much.

Only when your suffering becomes acute do you begin to reflect on your current state. Suffering often forces you to see things from another perspective or provides you with the impetus to move in a new direction. *It serves as a reminder that even though life is sometimes painful and ugly, it is also temporary, beautiful, and wild.* When you've reached this stage in your struggles, you long for something different and begin to question yourself further:

1. Are you seeing the beauty in life?
2. Are you living your life to the fullest?
3. To heck with what the world wants from you—what do you have to give and are you giving it?
4. What do you want to do and are you doing it? If not, why not?
5. How could you live your life differently? What do you need to change?

Until this shift happens for you—until your pain finally grows strong enough to compel you to change—you will find yourself agreeing with other people's ideas instead of trusting your own mind and instincts. You will glom onto the latest trends and reach for tools outside yourself as a means to cope with your discontent.

Trying to Ease the Pain—Your Genie in a Bottle

Americans don't like to stay stuck in their discontent; we are resourceful folks, so we take charge. We demand answers and implement quick fixes to make our lives more pleasurable. We have an affair. We take something to give us more energy during the day and something to help us sleep at night. We change jobs. We clamor for the next upgrade in technology, then waste countless hours in front of the television or computer screen. We adopt the latest eating trend, the latest health fad. In other words, we find a thousand ways to distract ourselves from our underlying discontent.

The problem is, these whims and quick fixes only promise pleasure; they don't bring true, lasting joy—just as alcohol promises temporary relief from pain or anxiety, television promises mindless escape, and money promises false security. All these things foster the illusion of happiness—and then that illusion quickly fades. Such is the cycle of discontent and self-soothing we find ourselves caught up in, only to repeat it over and over again.

Several years ago, my son said to me, "Mom, you're an alcoholic too, you just don't drink." He was right. We are all addicts to a certain degree in that most of us have a few cherished tools we like to use to help handle what life dishes out.

When I went through my divorce, I definitely drank more alcohol than usual to cope with the pain. I felt better for a short while, but then I just got tired.

When medical marijuana became available, I got a prescription for it to cope with the bad menstrual cramps I had suffered from my whole life. But truth be told, the cramps were really just a good excuse for me to get something legally that might lessen the fear that kept me paralyzed and unable to function well. I desperately wanted relief from the ache in my chest, the rapid beating of my heart, and the chaos in my mind. But the pot didn't work for the cramps, nor did it numb my pain. Instead, it made me feel paranoid, which was way worse than the original emotional pain I'd felt. The point is, I was trying to find something *outside* myself to help me feel better—a coping mechanism. And even if the marijuana had worked, it would only have offered temporary relief.

Of course, indulging a bit can certainly be enjoyable. Feeling a little looser after one margarita helped me to relax and to remember what it felt like to smile and laugh again. *But neither alcohol nor marijuana made me any happier the next day if I wasn't happy to begin with.* For that, I needed something much greater to happen *within* me. I needed to learn that I still had worth and that my existence on this planet was of value.

How can we recognize our own worth if we cover up who we really are with artificial substances, frenetic activities, and a panoply of coping behaviors? How can we appreciate or even utilize our gifts and talents if we fail to acknowledge them or bury them by distraction?

The Coping Mechanisms of Everyday People

Through my own struggles, I've been forced to learn about the addictions and afflictions we all confront—about individual frailties and the various ways we try to manage the unmanageable.

Many of us stay stuck in this place for a long time. Perhaps we are simply not unhappy *enough* to put forth the extra effort needed to make a change. Or maybe we don't know what to change or we change the wrong things. As a result, we continue to underestimate our own worth and hover through life at a low-energy level. We find strange comfort in our particular ruts because we know them so very well.

Listed here are some of the many behavioral grooves we fall into as we attempt to mitigate our emptiness and loneliness, our fear and uncertainty. A good number of these responses are perfectly acceptable in our culture. Some are even glorified, such as working extreme hours to prove our importance, so there may not be much impetus to abandon them. These strategies often serve as acceptable ways to disguise deeper issues and feelings we may not wish to confront—or those we aren't even aware of at the time. We mistakenly think they will help us be the person we'd really like to be or save us from exposing the person we fear we are. Our own delusions about our perceived worth (and our self-hatred) drive much of this process.

1. **Busyness/drama/chaos/excitement:** Indulging in behaviors such as impulsive actions that create an adrenaline rush; Internet surfing and constant texting; procrastinating and pushing deadlines; overscheduling activities and commitments; cleaning excessively; and pursuing extreme exercise and sports. Busyness often provides an excuse to avoid change.

2. **Power trips/competition/manipulation/self-righteousness:** Creating a false perception, for the benefit of others, about who you are (that is, crafting a substitute self—more on this later); thinking you are superior (in your religious and political beliefs, parenting techniques, job title, bank accounts, material possessions, athletic ability, educational level, and so on); and doing things for the wrong reasons (to hurt or control someone or to gain an advantage over another). Blaming others for your troubles and taking no accountability for your actions.

3. **Incorrect perceptions and judgments of others and ourselves:** Believing, for instance, that all men are bullies, all women are out for money, or all singles over fifty are damaged. You tell yourself, "She's got the perfect body (and I don't)" or "He's a trust fund baby (and I'm not)," which translates to, "I'm not as good and I don't deserve anything extraordinary, just a life of drudgery." The underlying misperception here is that your worth derives from circumstances outside yourself.

4. **Misusing substances:** Inappropriately consuming substances including (but not limited to) illegal, recreational, and prescribed drugs (antidepressants, sleep medications, painkillers, performance enhancers, marijuana, and the like); caffeine; sugar; junk food; energy drinks; and alcohol.

5. **Mishandling money:** Taking extreme positions on money and spending—wastefully, mindlessly spending significant sums on material goods (clothes, a bigger house, a nicer car, jewelry, electronics, and more) or, conversely, accumulating and excessively hoarding money for fear of losing it.

6. **Violence in the media and music:** Listening to or purchasing degrading music; adopting or emulating a glamorized gangster and gun mentality; and, through your media choices, supporting the perpetuation of violence on TV, in movies, and in video games. Growing numb to the escalating brutality in the media and identifying with the false sense of power it conveys.

7. **Outsourcing everything:** Having others, paid or not, mow your lawn, manicure your nails, shop for your groceries, prepare your meals, clean

your house, wash your car, do your fix-it jobs, tend your garden, groom your pet, and tackle a host of other tasks people used to do for themselves. You outsource the simple jobs that once created a feeling of accomplishment when you did them yourself. You may even outsource your God: you want a religious or spiritual person to tell you what you should believe and how you should pray, dress, and conduct yourself. Similarly, you want a doctor to diagnose your many ailments and give you prescriptions to make things better instead of taking your health into your own hands.

Of course, there are some jobs you need to hire out because you really don't have the time, because you strongly dislike doing them, or because you don't have the requisite knowledge or skill to complete them. However, when you outsource everything because you just don't want to do anything—or because it signifies that you've reached a certain social status—it doesn't necessarily result in improved well-being or in more enjoyment.

You miss out on the creativity and fulfillment that goes along with taking care of things and learning how to do new tasks—the feeling of accomplishment and contentment that comes when you complete a job or create something beautiful.

8. **Conforming by withholding personal expression:** Failing to honor and express your personality for fear of being judged by others. Holding back your natural tendencies in order to conform. Not fully trusting that your personality, your nuances, and individuality have merit and charm. You don't have to go over the top here to remedy things. Perhaps when you go to work, you might wear bold-colored shirts, ties, or scarves along with your business suits; when you go to exercise classes, you might don clothes that flow instead of being skintight and confining. You can make your hair a different color—or decide not to color it at all and let it go gray or silver or white as you age. These little freedoms of expression help you connect with your natural inclinations; they draw you out from the roles you often get stuck in. You feel more alive and energized when you can express your individuality instead of trying to blend in and hide your uniqueness. *There is a big difference between expressing individuality as an extension of yourself and trying to create an image you think will gain you social acceptance, recognition, or power.*

?.. Do you find yourself identifying with any of these behavior patterns or characteristics? Can you see how they'd work on a short-term basis only? Can you see how they might hinder you, or how blending into a purée of human sameness can dull your brightness?

Many of the activities or behaviors just listed won't affect your daily ability to perform in a normal capacity, or cause harm in limited doses. It is when you continually turn to them to deal with the harshness of life that they can backfire on you.

Most coping mechanisms are "easy," which is why we like them. They're convenient and quick fixes that offer fast relief. However, since the relief is temporary, you continually need more. You require more of the same remedy, and if that doesn't work or isn't possible, you switch to another mechanism altogether.

You may want to *feel* something—particularly to feel better or, as many describe it, to feel "alive." Or paradoxically, you may not want to feel anything at all because things are just too painful. In reality, it is far easier to take a pill and forget about your pain rather than to deal with it, especially if you are physically and emotionally worn out.

Adopting a New Approach

It's time to alter your approach. Your loved one's unmanageability has affected you deeply. It has distorted your thinking, damaged your sense of worth, and left unbelievably difficult situations at your doorstep. Simply put, *your* life has become unmanageable as well.

Trying to mold yourself according to society's rules and striving for success as defined by the American Dream have proven impossible goals. Meanwhile, you've found that your behavioral grooves and coping mechanisms no longer work. What may have succeeded for you in the past can no longer hold everything together. You have little peace in the present and scant hope for the future.

You've reached your breaking point. Longing for relief, you sincerely desire a new way of life. And you are finally willing to seek it in a different place—perhaps a place you hadn't even thought of before. The good news is that you won't have to search far, for that place lies *within you.*

4

Confronting
the Real Problem

Mistaken Identity

You suffer from mistaken identity. You don't fully comprehend your worth exactly as you are, nor do others because they also feel judged. Consider all the forms of judgment that exist in our world, involving issues as diverse as race, religion, being gay or transgendered, addiction, mental illness, educational level, earning capacity, language skill, beauty and weight, and athleticism. When you don't feel you have inherent worth, everyone else becomes competition. As a result, you live in a state of containment and resignation, quietly accepting your lack of the attributes your society prizes highly. Alternatively, you may find yourself constantly striving to attain and maintain those same qualities, unable to find contentment within your own natural state.

How do you garner the courage to go your own direction, let your light shine, and contribute your significance to the world in a way that only you can do if you constantly undervalue your importance and minimize your attributes and achievements? The answer is, you don't. Instead, you conform and adopt coping mechanisms. Meanwhile, you feel as if something is missing, and you continue to wonder what your purpose is and why you're here.

You'll never know your purpose if you don't first recognize and accept the value of your own life. How can you offer yourself to the world in purpose if you don't feel you have anything to give? The issue of self-worth doesn't just apply to addicts and alcoholics. It applies as well to all those who love them and to anyone else who feels a lack of personal value and connection with others.

The Loss of Identity and How It Happens

"You seem to have lost your original identity and have identified with your thoughts and body. Suppose I ask you who you are if you don't identify with anything whatsoever. If you say, 'I am a man,' you have identified yourself with a masculine body. If you say, 'I am a professor,' you are identifying with the ideas gathered in your brain. If you say, 'I am a millionaire,' you are identifying with your bank account; if 'a mother,' with a child; 'a husband,' with a wife. 'I am tall; I am short; I am black or white' shows your identification with the color and shape of the body. But without any identifications, who are you? Have you ever thought about it? When you really understand that, you will see we are all the same. If you detach yourself completely from all the things you have identified yourself with, you realize yourself as the pure 'I.' In that pure 'I' there is no difference between you and me. ... That is why, if we could calm our minds and get to the basis of all these modifications, we would find the unity among everything. ... Only then can we love our neighbors as our own Self. Otherwise, how is it possible? If I identify myself with my body, I will also see another person as a body and the two bodies cannot be one—they are always different. If I identify myself with my mind, nobody can have a mind exactly like mine. ... But behind all these differences, in the Self, we never differ. That means behind all these ever-changing phenomena is a never changing One. ..."

—The Yoga Sutras of Patanjali,
commentary on Sutra 1:4 by Swami Satchidananda

I recognized myself in this reading (for the full text of this passage, see Appendix A). It had a tremendous impact on me. I saw that I had spent my whole life trying to define myself according to societal standards and messages I received from outside myself. I perfected my acting skills, convinced that if I did everything I thought others expected from the role I was playing, I would be accepted and would find my place and purpose in the universe. The only problem was, it didn't work. By trying to identify with or actually adopt certain roles, I prevented my own unique path from unfolding.

When you don't feel you have inherent worth, everyone else becomes competition.

I acted as if I felt worthy when I really didn't. I thought I was greater than or less than others based on my accomplishments, my children's achievements, my income and education, my popularity, and so forth. I built myself up by doing more, always more, or by putting others down. I spent so much time trying to learn my lines and maintain my perceived roles (adopted child, wife, ex-wife, mother of a drug addict, middle-class citizen, rescuer, fixer) that I locked away my heart and soul and stifled my true feelings. Small wonder that I felt so alone, ungrounded, and misaligned.

If you feel this way prior to dealing with a loved one's addiction, then the space between your role and your soul will grow bigger still as you try to handle an even greater role—that of managing someone else's life.

?.. What roles have you played in your lifetime? What roles are you trying to fulfill right now?

Borrowed Beliefs and the Substitute Self

When you are young, you gain insight into yourself from the influences of the people and situations that surround you. Your religious affiliations, manners, moral values, racial attitudes, eating patterns, and political preferences are taught to you; none of these characteristics are innate.

Had you been born in another country or into another family of origin, your perspectives would no doubt be quite different. Various cultures prize different outward appearances and practice different customs and religions; many don't treat people of all races, genders, and sexual orientations equally. Cuisines, work environments, family dynamics, and other societal norms vary from one nation to the next. Even within the United States, many variations depend on geographic location.

As you grow up, you continue to develop your identity based partially on perceptions you form from the feedback others give you. Layer upon layer, the ongoing social conditioning shapes your identity—your notions of who you are, how others see you, how you in turn see them, and where you seem to fit within your particular corner of the globe. If this social conditioning feels comfortable to you at a deep level, you are fortunate and probably have a healthy grasp on your identity. Eventually, that identity will become the lens through which you view the world.

If, however, circumstances force you to adopt an identity contrary to your true self—perhaps as a means of protection or because of your own naïveté—it can cause great internal conflict. This misidentification becomes your "substitute self."

An Example of a Substitute Self:
My First Insight into Who and What I Thought I Was

·{ MY STORY }·

A pivotal moment for me came as I was riding my bicycle when I was around nine. I was heading home at the end of the day when the strangest thought popped into my head, "What if I'm adopted?"

My mom had mentioned that she wanted to talk with me after dinner that evening. I was pondering what she might have to say, feeling a little concerned. After all, she'd *never* set up an appointment to speak with me before. "What if I'm adopted?" I repeated to myself as I walked into the house for dinner.

After the dishes were cleared, my mother sat down with me on my bed (the top bunk, since I was the oldest and got first choice). I was stunned as I heard her say, "Did you know you were adopted?" Then she broke down in tears and asked me if I could ever forgive her. I started crying too in sympathy. I didn't understand what was going on.

That evening, she explained that she had been raped and became pregnant with me as a result. And over and over again, she whispered that she was so *terribly* sorry. I vaguely knew what rape was, but I couldn't comprehend why she was asking for my forgiveness.

Meanwhile, my young brain began connecting the dots. "Thank goodness I wasn't *totally* adopted," I reasoned. At least I had one parent who was biologically mine. And that meant that my favorite set of grandparents, the ones on my mom's side, were really mine too. Phew!

She didn't tell her parents about the rape for a long time. She thought her dad would get mad at her for accepting a ride from a stranger, so she harbored all the guilt, fear, and shame she felt until it became apparent that she was pregnant. She could no longer hide her growing belly.

The family's reaction was probably typical for the era. My grandparents—my two favorite people in the world during my childhood—had wanted her to give me up for adoption. But she chose to keep me, defying their wishes. As was common in those days, she was sent away to give birth.

Instead of feeling grateful that my mother wanted me enough to go against her parents' wishes, my nine-year-old self focused on the thought that my grandparents, the two grounding influences in my life, *didn't want her to keep me.*

At that time, I couldn't comprehend why they thought it would be best to give me up for adoption. That my mother was only sixteen, would get no help from the biological father, and wasn't out of high school yet didn't seem to matter to me. And the fact that my mom decided to keep me didn't even *begin* to register in my mind as the heroic act it was. Instead, I got lost in a confusing new description of myself: I was unplanned, a mistake, unwanted, different. She was seventeen when she gave birth to me. That conversation on my bunk bed altered my life and changed my fundamental sense of who I was. I went from feeling like a normal, loved child to feeling that I had to prove my value in order to justify my existence; I had to show the world that I had been worth keeping and that my mom had made the right decision.

Suddenly, I felt different from my little brother and sister. Unlike me, they had the same parents and the same grandparents. They were planned and wanted. I felt less than equal.

My thinking and behavior changed from that point on, and a pattern emerged that would only become more entrenched over time. I refused to accept mediocrity in anything I did. As I saw it, I couldn't *afford* to be mediocre. It might jeopardize my merit in the eyes of my family and the world at large. I carried that trait with me for many, many years (to be honest, I still fall back into the pattern from time to time). Heck, one day I wet my pants standing in the front of my grade school classroom when I had to pee badly but didn't want to lose a spelling contest. My teacher graciously got some paper towels to clean up the floor without saying a thing to embarrass me. On my walk home for lunch that day, the defiant Wyoming wind blew my pants dry, so I never told my mother about the incident. It would've been too humiliating. Instead, I went back to school after lunch wearing the same pants.

This story goes to show how events in our lives, especially in our formative years, can cause us to think of ourselves as something we're not and as someone we don't need to be. My grandparents didn't know me, of course, back when they were making what they thought was a wise decision for their pregnant daughter—but I'm happy to say they ended up crazy in love with me not long after.

The same thing happened with the man I've always called "Dad." He married my mom when I was seven months old and adopted me shortly thereafter. As far as he was concerned, I was his child. He loved me like his own and always treated me as an equal to my younger brother and sister. I never suffered from a lack of love. He gave me an incredible life.

The key point is this: the misperceptions you create in your mind become the stories you tell yourself over and over again as you move through life. What's more, the mental baggage you carry around becomes heavier with each retelling of these tales. And as long as the old stories are weighing you down, your true value will remain obscured, your unique potential untapped.

If you can't identify these misperceptions and change your thinking, the untruths can lead you into a false sense of self, culminating in wrong career choices, unhealthy relationships, and destructive lifestyles.

The Chief Obstacle to Happiness

Perhaps the most destructive of all human tendencies doesn't readily come to mind. Certainly, consuming drugs and alcohol is harmful and potentially deadly for an addict, but most damaging of all is the deeper, causal thought process that occurs in some people and can foster, and later exacerbate, addiction—the underlying, deep-seated disbelief in their intrinsic value as human beings. As a result, they turn to things outside themselves, such as substances or actions, to ease their discomfort, cope with their sense of inadequacy and self-loathing, and attempt to feel normal. Some of these individuals may have seemed fine before suffering a traumatic event or before a painkiller was prescribed to them. But then, addiction put a stranglehold on them, sapping whatever personal power and self-worth they once had. (Mind you, I'm not talking about people with mental illness. That's a whole different issue not addressed in this book.)

As one who loves an addict, you may often find their lack of self-worth even sadder than their actual use of drugs and alcohol. You cannot comprehend how they could possibly think so little of themselves that they would bring so much pain and punishment into their life, especially when you know just how amazing they really are.

But think about your reaction here. You are engaging in a similar thought process, are you not? Just as they look to drugs, alcohol, pornography, or food to provide them a measure of relief, you look to them to provide *your* relief—you use their recovery as a prerequisite for your own happiness. Put another way, you need them to be okay in order to be okay yourself. Your life has become dependent on their well-being, just as they are dependent on their drug of choice.

If you're a parent, you're used to sacrificing many things for the best interests of your child. If you could take away their pain by absorbing it yourself, you would. In fact, you already have: you've driven yourself crazy, turned your world upside down, and most likely spent a ton of money in an effort to save them. Your substitute self is the "fixer" or "rescuer." You've pleaded, yelled, enabled, and cried to get them to stop the devastation. Yet their pain persists.

When none of your tireless, heroic actions work, it's normal to question your own worth. After all, if you can't make life better for your child, then what is your purpose as a parent? What right do you have to live a good life when they're suffering and you're unable to help?

The truth is, you have every right. You deserve to be well, even if your loved one isn't, and you deserve to be happy, even if they aren't. You don't need to punish yourself because you weren't able to help them get better. You are not that powerful. You cannot control the uncontrollable—another person's choices. It is sad but true.

In adulthood, life becomes a great (and often harsh) teacher. Poor choices elicit consequences that serve as a far better deterrent than your personal coercion ever could.

Both parties, you and your addicted loved one, actually suffer from the same basic malady—an inability to understand that your specific, individual life has impact, value, and significance. Be assured that your life has purpose and meaning—but it cannot be used to mandate the choices your loved one makes. Otherwise, you will lose the connection with your personal power, and your well-being will hinge upon your addict following your advice (which they rarely do). *You must believe that your life is worth saving just as much as theirs is, or else there will be two people giving their power away by not taking control of their own actions and reactions.*

In the yoga world, this obstacle—this failure to recognize and honor one's own worth—is referred to as "ignorance," and it is said to lie at the root of all afflictions. To be described as ignorant in this context does *not* mean you are stupid. Quite the contrary: it means you ignore or are unaware of your own significance. And that, as we have seen, can have serious consequences, for yourself and those you love.

... you need them to be okay in order to be okay yourself. Your life has become dependent on their well-being, just as they are dependent on their drug of choice.

Are You Living in Fear or Freedom?

When you don't love yourself or believe you have worth, fear will creep in—fear that you aren't good enough or that something will go wrong regardless of your intentions. Fear is, of course, a natural human response, but too much of it can be debilitating, even devastating. Loving an addict often means conjuring up terrible images of outcomes that could happen as a result of the choices they make. And that, in turn, can cause you to become ill-tempered and irrational, no matter how smart, even-keeled, and sensible you have been in the past. No law of nature dictates that your fears will be realized. Things don't have to turn out the way you've always worried about; in fact, they likely have just as much chance of turning out well. But sometimes, it's difficult to get past your own fearful reasoning.

Fear Causes Resistance to Life: It Hijacks Hope and Potential

If you exist in a fearful state, you approach life in a defensive manner, unable to live freely, take risks, let go of outcomes, and make mistakes. Your misperception of your own worth paralyzes you and impedes your ability to expand your own well-being and brilliance.

Because of fear, you manifest behavioral flaws—reactions and traits you adopt as protective measures to safeguard you from the bad things you envision. But instead, these flaws actually keep you wound up in a tight ball of unexpressed potential.

If fear is causing you to continually resist life, you may find yourself engaged in one or more of the following behaviors:

• **Becoming too dependent on certain people or things** (examples include addictive substances, coping mechanisms, and expected outcomes). You may want things done a specific way, or perhaps you want things to stay the same forever; thus, you might stay in a job you hate for years just because you're afraid of what a change might do to your life—after all, things could turn out even worse!
• **Resenting others and blaming others for your own unhappiness.** You blame everyone and everything for your circumstances, since that's easier than looking at yourself in the mirror and making changes. You play the victim, but even though you might get some sympathy in the process, remember this: you can never be your own hero as long as you

remain a victim. The hero and the victim cannot coexist. Blaming others robs you of your personal power.

- **Comparing yourself to others.** You constantly judge yourself and others, picking winners and losers—and act accordingly, adopting an air of superiority, on one hand, or becoming overwhelmed by self-disgust, on the other. As Theodore Roosevelt observed, "Comparison is the thief of joy."

I've heard it said that fear is energy rooted in your ego, where the chaos in your mind primarily occurs. Love, by contrast, is energy that comes from your soul—the deeper, wiser, and everlasting part of you. When you live in fear, all the decisions you make stem from fear. *Fear displaces hope and limits potential.* Living in fear brings a disproportionate amount of worry into your life, which then only reinforces your fear-based actions. Building a life on self-love is the antidote.

Primary Fears That Cause Imbalance

To regain a sense of balance, you must begin to remove or replace some of your fears. If you don't, you will remain lopsided. You'll squander your time trying to manipulate and manage uncontrollable situations because you're uncomfortable with life having its own way, which it always will. Strangely enough, you might not realize that you have a too-fearful nature. Indeed, you may pride yourself on how dedicated, strong, and resilient you are by trying to resist life in the first place.

Here is a list of the primary fears that most people experience. The vast majority of other, more specific fears fall into one of these four broad categories:

1. **You fear you are inadequate and that your defects will be exposed.** You are inherently flawed in some way, or you will make a mistake that proves you're stupid, abnormal, unworthy, or the like.
2. **You fear you won't get something you think you need.** This would be a specific outcome you seek—for instance, control over a person or situation, such as a loved one's sobriety; a job promotion; or acceptance by others.
3. **You fear you will lose something that you already have.** This might include, for example, financial security, physical health or beauty, a relationship, a job title, or simple peace of mind.

4. You fear that you will end up alone—that you will die alone and no one will care. Curiously, all the other fears end up in this category at some point. That is, if any of the other three fears are realized, you'll be afraid you'll wind up unloved, unaccepted, alone, unwanted, uncared for, and disposable. To illustrate, consider the fear of spiders. Typically, the fear is that they'll jump on you, crawl all over you, bite you, ravage your body and maybe even eat you, cause a panic attack, or bring on a heart attack—and you will be helpless to stop them. You'll probably be alone at the time, and you may die alone as a result. By the way, did I mention that not all fears are rational?

?

.. Try thinking of some of the things you are most afraid of— can you see which category they fit into?

Many specific fears are manufactured and imaginary, and facing them down is often a good way to conquer them. When you're in the grips of a particular fear, remember this acronym: FEAR = False Expectations Appearing Real. It is a reminder that your current fears aren't immediately true, that you're worrying over imagined outcomes that may never occur, and that it's okay to let go of these kinds of fears.

One essential truth about life is that you cannot control it. Nor can you avoid tragedy, no matter how carefully you manage your life. But always keep in mind that you are free to enjoy peace and love even as you confront heartache and serious difficulties. Here's an insight I treasure: *joy and tragedy can happen concurrently.* Thus, for example, even if your loved one refuses to communicate with you, you can still enjoy the blessing of having a job that you love. It doesn't have to be one or the other. Gratitude for the good things can exist alongside sadness for the unfortunate ones.

·{MY STORY}·

When I was in the beginning phase of my divorce, my children's father took them to his annual family reunion. I was miserable. It was the first time I had missed one of those gatherings since we began dating nearly twenty years earlier. Moreover, I knew his family members would all find out during this occasion that we were ending our marriage: the consequences of divorce were beginning to hit me. I felt terribly lonely while my boys were gone and didn't know what to do with my free time, since I didn't usually have much of it. One day, I decided to eat lunch at a nearby Chinese restaurant. When my first course arrived, a simple yet amazing thought entered my mind: "I can still enjoy hot and sour soup!" What a revelation that was. Just minutes before, I had felt as though my life was falling apart, yet here was something that lifted my spirits and brought a smile to my face. Hooray! At least in that small moment, my life wasn't just doom and gloom after all.

There are times when it is hard to remember what joy feels like, such as when your loved one (and therefore you) are in the middle of a terrible situation and your fears turn out to be real. (See "A Three-Rule Approach for Crisis Survival", chapter 9.) Trying to mitigate, understand, and deal with any repercussions consumes your time and energy. It can be nearly impossible to view the future with any hope when you are filled with despair. You might wonder, as I did, why this is happening to you and your loved one, or perhaps you feel jealous of those families around you who appear to have a "normal" life. In these moments, you long for something, anything that will make your situation different.

When you're in the grips of a particular fear, remember this acronym: FEAR = False Expectations Appearing Real

This book exists to show you a different perspective on life and to remind you that no matter what is going on with your loved one, your life is not over nor are you destined to live in misery. Instead of endlessly wondering why the bad stuff is happening to you, you can employ the techniques in these pages to redirect your focus and discover a better way. Regardless of how bleak your situation looks today, the truth is that you *can* experience peace and joy once again. There is great hope for your future.

5

The 3 Rs for the Soul: The First R—Rethinking Religion and Your Inherent Worth

An Overview of the 3 Rs—
Rethinking, Reclaiming, and Releasing

Your personal presence is the most important thing you possess. It is the combination of energy and light that radiates from your soul into everything you do. It embodies your very essence, and no one can take it from you. It will never leave you—although *you* may abandon *it* through denial, misperception, and suppression.

The good news is that you can always return to it: the only thing necessary to reclaim your personal presence is your willingness to do so. The work is simple but not easy. Check your ego at the door and be prepared to learn some fascinating things during this journey of the self.

By implementing the "3 Rs for the Soul" that I'll discuss in this and the next two chapters—centered on rethinking, reclaiming, and releasing—you'll learn how to live with power, purpose, and passion by developing these vital attributes:

- **A strong, individual spiritual connection, perhaps unlike anything you've ever experienced**
- **The personal power to maintain and protect your well-being regardless of external circumstances, and**
- **The freedom to live your life with less fear and regret**

The First R: Rethinking

Claiming your spiritual power is the most critical element in your transformation. It is the foundation that will enable you to live and act from a place of trust—trust in something greater than yourself that will guide your life. With your spiritual power renewed, you will come to see that something far more intelligent than any human is at work within the universe, and you will feel a desire to align yourself with it. *This realization can occur in the context of any religion—or with no religion at all.* Organized faith doesn't work for everyone, and in my experience, it can actually stunt spiritual growth when used incorrectly, as I'll discuss later.

It doesn't matter what your particular beliefs entail. However, if you don't believe you have inherent worth and/or if your current spiritual practice hasn't brought you closer to God (or some Higher Guidance, whatever that is for you), then what you are doing now clearly is not working. By rethinking and challenging your religious dogma, you will learn where your personal spiritual quest and practices are failing you. Then you can work to strengthen them and thereby bring greater fulfillment into your life.

The Second R: Reclaiming

Your personal power endows you with the ability to stand up for yourself and make choices that neither hinder nor harm your unique potential. Among other things, this includes the capacity to change or remove the current obstacles on your path and to create boundaries that protect you from the actions and behaviors of others. When you begin to understand and believe in your inherent worth (the first R), this aspect of your life will be greatly enhanced.

The Third R: Releasing

Once you have worked on the first and second Rs, releasing your essence becomes a natural by-product. Your personal expression will emanate from your spiritual self instead of from a substitute self—the guise you may have maintained to fit into the role you previously played. You are done with that now. There is no need to continue the charade. Instead, you welcome your unique gifts and talents and find that sharing them with the world is not only natural but also liberating and fulfilling.

Whether this sharing takes place within the context of a career, a pastime, or a relationship doesn't matter. What is important is that you become a conduit for love and support for others. You no longer hold back and adhere to self-imposed or societal boundaries. You trust more and fear less. You release your radiance and energy into the world with abandon.

?

.. How strong is your personal presence? Do you feel that you have inherent worth? Or are you constantly asking yourself, "How do I fit in, what is my purpose, and why do I exist?"

The First R: Rethinking Your Religious and Spiritual Beliefs

Did you know you can fire your current God? Yes, you can. Note that I did not say do away with God; actually, my meaning is quite the contrary.

But why would anyone fire their God? you ask. Well, perhaps your original interpretation of God is flawed or simply false. In fact, some of your old beliefs and behaviors might be precisely what has kept you from establishing a real connection with a Higher Guidance.

Consider these questions. Have you lived your life with a fear of God that was instilled in you at some point? Have you felt shame, humiliation, and judgment for who you are and how you act (or fail to act)? Have you behaved as though you agree with everything a church espouses when you do not or tried to forge all your thoughts and behaviors into a specific religious model in order to fit in or to make it to heaven? If your answer to any of these questions is yes, then it's likely you haven't been able to come into your own passionate self, fully capable of free expression in the world.

You know *about* God, but that is quite different from knowing God. And if you don't really know God and, as an extension, don't fully understand your worth and what you can offer to the world, you're missing the point of existence.

Does It Have to Be Called God?

No. Your Higher Guidance can be called anything you want. I choose to call it God, but you can decide what name works best for you. I've heard it referred to by a wide variety of names, among them Higher Power, Divinity, Source, Universal Energy, Light, Spirit, Nature, Love, Goodness, Wisdom, the Higher Self, and the Oversoul. It doesn't even need to be named or defined; it just can't be you, or the lower self (ego), which we'll get into later. I'll use different terms throughout the book. Feel free to replace my words with your own. Please don't get hung up on the verbiage, or, again, you'll miss the point.

I don't define it or claim to have it all figured out. What makes sense to me is that there's something at work in the universe that I cannot fully comprehend or explain. To me, that means there is something much bigger and more powerful than me at work, an intelligence more advanced than my own. It's that simple.

Why Seek Out This Connection?

If you love an alcoholic or addict, you may well be in need of something powerful in which to place your trust. Much of your faith has been diminished:

you've lost faith in your addict, faith in your ability to change their behavior or manage your own at times, and faith that God still cares about you or your addicted loved one. You may feel so broken that the only shred of hope you have left is that there is something more out there. Otherwise, you see no sense or purpose to this thing called life. If ever there was a time to rekindle or re-create a spiritual connection, it is now.

The Spiritual Omnivore

One of the coolest things about living in America is that we have freedom of religion. We get to choose how we believe, what we believe, and even *if* we believe.

Contrary to what many of us may have understood or been taught in the past, however, we don't have to be confined to one school of religious thought, thereby forsaking all other spiritual concepts and practices.

At first, I was terrified to question my religion. As stupid as it sounds, I almost expected the proverbial bolt of lightning to come down and strike me. I thought really bad things would begin happening at any moment. It was as if I was turning my back on God, when in reality, I wanted to be *closer* to God. I was more afraid of the "devil" getting ahold of me than I was of feeling disconnected.

Instead, I found tremendous freedom as I pursued a way to satisfy a spiritual longing that had truly never been filled, one where I wasn't afraid to have my own views even if they differed from those of a particular institution or person. I realized I didn't need to flaunt such views, have others agree with them, or even talk about them. But neither would I deny them anymore.

I find it so liberating to learn about different practices, and over time, I have personally adopted certain new ways of thinking and dismissed others—without guilt. I continue to be open to fresh information and other interpretations. I'm constantly amazed at the limits that I had previously placed upon myself.

It is easy to get stuck in worn-out beliefs and patterns of behaving and thinking that no longer serve you. This can occur in all sorts of areas—your religious views, parenting techniques, gender roles, exercise regimens, or eating preferences, to cite just a few. For instance, have you driven yourself crazy over the years trying to conform to the latest eating fad—vegan, vegetarian, dairy free, gluten free, paleo, no sugar, no carbs, no fat, whatever?

You don't have to do this! You can be an omnivore instead! You can love Jesus and also agree with some of the Buddha's principles. You can eat a mainly vegetarian diet and enjoy an occasional steak. You can incorporate yoga philosophy and the Twelve Steps as well as Jewish mysticism into your life. I've read in mystical Indian readings that *a God defined is a God confined*. You don't have to fit inside a premade box—and don't let anyone tell you differently. Work with what feels right for your soul, not just for the sake of convenience or for anyone else's sake. Take your spirituality into your own hands so that it can support and guide you.

If you have a chosen religion, you may opt to stick with it but take a greater role in your connection with God: if you find certain discordant elements in your religion, don't let that preclude you from establishing a strong spiritual connection. Or perhaps you could work for change within your religion rather than dismissing its value out of hand.

Possibly, you will find that disagreement with fundamental principles is a major stumbling block in your relationship to God. Living with the conflict between your views and your religion's views may prove too much to handle. If you believe in gay rights, for example, you will not be able to attend a church that condemns homosexuality. If you believe a woman has the right to control her own body, you won't want to attend a church that condemns abortion. Thus, you may begin distancing yourself from your religion or leaving it entirely. But what of your relationship with God? Did you leave God also?

It is critical to be honest with yourself about what you really believe and feel to be true. Even slight dishonesty will keep you at odds, feeling stuck between what you profess to believe in public and what you know in your heart to be your true beliefs.

When you don't acknowledge the pieces you disagree with and instead push them into deep, dark crevices inside yourself, the underlying conflict never goes away. It just gets covered up. And in time, those hidden pieces become impediments on your path toward a spiritually liberating life. Every little personal truth you deny, ignore, or hide away leaves a hole in the fabric of your well-being. And like bits of sand thrown against the hardest rock by centuries of wind, these tiny pieces ultimately will erode the very foundation of your spirituality.

How can you find the truth in anything if you can't first find it within yourself? How can you hope to uncover or reclaim your passion, gifts, and talents in life if they're lying dormant, mired in the misperceptions you continue to embrace? How can you hope to align with any deeper knowledge of your purpose if you aren't first acting from a place of deep truth? When you don't confront misperception, the problem just gets bigger.

Once you shine a light on some of your hidden thoughts and feelings and acknowledge their existence, you are then able to set them and yourself free. The more you align yourself with your own truth, the closer you will come to connecting with a Higher Guidance. The universe will begin to support you, and you will finally be able to tap into a power much greater than any you've previously known. You will be able to hop onto an energy groove that is more consistent with your soul. Until then, however, you will continue to live based on the borrowed beliefs of others, beliefs that eventually will cease to sustain you and instead stunt your growth. But know this: you do not have to settle for crumbs when there is so much more. You can choose to become a spiritual omnivore!

?..If you are settling for crumbs within your spiritual practice, where else are you settling in your life? What are some of the things you've been pushing away in order to avoid dealing with them?

Are You Checking the Boxes and Then Checking Out?

Here are some of the typical thoughts and behaviors I witness among many people who identify with a specific religion, whether they currently attend church or not. Can you relate to any of these attitudes?

Some tell me, "I've identified with 'xyz' religion my whole life— and I will never change." Some people who tell me they believe in God go to church regularly, and some rarely attend a service. Yet their religious convictions (virtually from birth) can be so deeply embedded that to change them would be akin to cutting off an appendage. These people would rather walk past the mirror of religious reflection than look too deeply into it. They may thank Him at meals, give praise and gratitude when good things happen, worship Him on holidays, and pray when they need to. And they would never entertain the thought of changing their religious affiliation in order to experience a deeper connection to God. Period. (In rare cases, if these believers are faced with an excruciating life circumstance in which their religion fails them miserably they *might* question their faith.) They are more connected to their religious membership than they are to God.

Some declare, "I'm very religious." Ironically, people who ardently profess their faith are often the most closed off, spiritually, of all the people I meet. They can appear quite virtuous. They attend church regularly, might even be involved in ministry, and fulfill their church responsibilities with perfection. But when life gets dicey, their God isn't someone who brings them peace. These people can be quite lovely to know and are often very bright. They believe fervently in the *idea* of God. But their fundamental lack of trust in God often causes them to take matters into their own hands, leaving God behind. They drive themselves and others crazy trying to control everything and everyone around them. Many know how to kneel at the appropriate times, make the appropriate hand gestures, repeat the proper responses to a priest's words, and pray exactly as they've been taught. But they don't know how to experience God in all things: to trust and love God, to love themselves, and to love others.

Others tell me they have a punishing God. They think they are constantly being judged and feel guilt if they don't behave perfectly. When bad things happen, they wonder if they are being reprimanded. They always question themselves about what they did wrong and how they could've done things better; they continually beat themselves up and are filled with self-blame. I see this attitude a lot with the parents of alcoholics and drug addicts who consider themselves very religious. One phrase I've heard over and over again is, "I did everything I was supposed to do." *There is a false belief that perfect behavior ensures a perfect life.* This mindset keeps them locked in a pattern of striving, feeling they've failed, and then becoming more critical of themselves for not being perfect. When you feel judged by God, you tend to judge yourself, and in turn, you also judge others for failing to live up to your (higher) standards.

Some people say, "My personal actions outside church are a separate matter." These folks feel at odds with their religion when they engage in behaviors that are not condoned or encouraged by their church (such as having premarital sex, drinking alcohol, or seeking an abortion), so they hide such behaviors. Even though these matters may be no one else's business, they judge themselves immoral and are secretly filled with shame. They are deeply conflicted about acting one way in public and another way in private. This conflict creates a split in their identity, which fosters opposition and a splintered self. Nonetheless, they continue to play the pious role in order to maintain acceptance within their religious community.

·{ MY STORY }·

In my late thirties, I switched from one Christian church to another. My former church did not condone drinking alcohol: indeed, if you drank, you were not deemed worthy to attend services at the temple. The church I moved to had no such prohibition on drinking. It seemed so strange to me that two Christ-based institutions treated the matter so differently. It took me a while to rid myself of the guilt I felt about consuming alcohol after I joined my new church, even though I had enjoyed that freedom until I was thirty-five or so.

Did I suddenly become less worthy because I chose to have a margarita now and then? Granted, having too many margaritas could have distanced me from God and myself, but did abstaining from alcohol really bring me closer to Him? Put another way, does focusing on the minutiae of "appropriate" behavior (dressing modestly, say, or forgoing alcohol, caffeine, and tobacco) strengthen our spirituality? Or are we really just checking the boxes of appropriate behavior and then checking out? Do protocol and guilt get us closer to God? Only you can answer that question for yourself.

Making Other People or Things Your God.

Many people, often unknowingly, give away their power and place their happiness into the hands of a spouse, a church, a job, an addiction, or a loved one's addiction. This other entity then becomes their Higher Guidance, replacing God.

But it is key to recognize that even though people and things can *add* to your happiness, they cannot *be* your happiness. We are all responsible for discovering and perpetuating our own happiness. When you give part of yourself away to other people, groups, and things, God only gets the leftovers.

Some people feel resentful and don't know why. If your faith is fragile, it will inhibit how you move into life and within your world. You'll play it small and safe, accepting things just the way they are whether you like it or not. You'll stay stuck in old habits, wrong career choices, abusive situations, and so forth. Deep down, you may know that you deserve more, but you aren't sure how to get it. You might be afraid of the repercussions or afraid you'll fail if you try to make things different, so you remain stuck. Resentments build as you begrudgingly accept what life has given you instead of reaching for what life has in store for you by changing those things that you have the power to alter. You silently blame others when the person you are really most disappointed with is yourself.

Some people give up on God. You might've felt disgraced or lied to in the name of religion and want nothing more to do with it. Or perhaps you just flat out don't believe in religion or in a Higher Guidance. That's okay too. I have been in the position of wanting to wash my hands of religion, partly as a result of being reprimanded by one particular denomination (as I will mention shortly) but also because of a fundamental disconnect with some of its rules and beliefs. But even though you may not be perfectly happy with a specific religious institution or with your spiritual beliefs of old, it doesn't mean you necessarily need to drop either—especially if you are getting closer to God and fully believe in your inherent worth and live your life accordingly.

You may choose to change your religion or your beliefs, but there is a big difference between dumping religious or spiritual beliefs and dumping God. *You do not have to dump God.*

You Don't Have to Dump God

I would never be so deluded as to try to change anyone's beliefs. I'm not that powerful, nor would it be appropriate for me to do so. My beliefs and practices are mine alone. However, when I see people struggling with religion and spirituality just as I did, I'm happy to share my story and the insights I've gained on how to find your own spiritual connection. One of the first things to do is to reexamine your current and previously held beliefs.

… even though people and things can add to your happiness, they cannot be your happiness.

At the outset, you may be incredibly frightened to question your deep-seated religious beliefs or the long-standing traditions and patterns that have been passed down to you, even when they no longer serve your needs. I certainly was. It takes courage to examine and let go of things we never fully felt were right or true. It's much, much easier to look the other way. In certain situations, making a change means you risk losing some of your dearest relationships. At a minimum, it opens the door to uncertainty, potential ridicule, and possible rejection. It also means that you might experience a fair amount of ambiguity and insecurity for a while until you figure out just how the change in your belief system will affect your life. Sometimes, the only thing you know is that your current belief system isn't sustaining you. You don't trust it, nor are you aware of your worth. Simply admitting that is a very good way to start.

As you move forward, you will tend to react with fear. You may want to grab back the very beliefs that you've started to let go of, but don't allow panic to take over. Maintain the resolve to keep questioning and the willingness to be in a vulnerable place of uncertainty for a while. It's the only way you can change and grow. Otherwise, you will remain stagnant, which makes it darn near impossible to reach your greatest potential—or even handle your current problems in a better manner.

Assuming you're being honest, the more questions you ask yourself about what you truly believe, the more answers will come; bit by bit, a more accurate picture of who you are will emerge, and you will see just how you can incorporate fresh spiritual information into your daily life. The uneasiness lessens as you begin to step into your new and honest self. None of us has all the answers, but putting the pieces of your fragmented self back together gives you a much stronger foundation to build on as you move forward.

What I have witnessed time and time again is that when people truly connect with a Higher Guidance, they begin to comprehend their inherent worth and don't feel the need to go outside themselves to find it. This is when their lives take off.

?... Are you at odds with any of the beliefs you've been taught? Do they help you feel free to express who you really are without shame or judgment?

Beginning a New Spiritual Journey

My spiritual path took a turn when I failed to live up to the standards of the church I was attending. I had committed a sin in the church's eyes, and my transgression warranted corrective action (that is, punitive consequences).

·{ MY STORY }·

In my midthirties and when my kids were in elementary and middle school, I attended a Christian church whose emphasis was on the family. I loved that aspect of it. This particular religion was new to me, so I tried to learn everything I could from observing the other members, in hopes of fitting in.

I molded myself around what I perceived as the right way to act, speak, and dress in this church community: I tithed, prayed using their specific terminology, abstained from coffee and alcohol, served in various positions as requested, maintained the role of a "good woman" and "good mom" by wearing modest clothing and cooking more, put my kids in Boy Scouts and piano lessons, switched their school, and wore the obligatory dress for females on Sundays. I loved the community aspect of the church. I had many church friends, as did my children, and we felt very supported. No one *made* me do any of this. It appeared to be good for all of us, so I happily obliged.

I disagreed with some of the church's fundamental principles, but that didn't seem to matter. I wasn't actively involved in any opposing causes, nor did any of the contradictions affect me personally at the time. It was easy to overlook and dismiss any discrepancies. And then I hit a bump in the road that threw everything up in the air.

I had hoped that the emphasis on family would help to keep my own family intact. Having thought about divorce previously, I was optimistic that this church experience would help us stay together and that it would be beneficial for all of us. It was, for a while. We were all distracted with new friends and church activities. But the problems never really went away. They just got pushed aside.

After filing for divorce some time later, I had a brief relationship with someone I had met in another state. At that point, I wasn't feeling too good about myself; the divorce process had been traumatic, and I felt pretty beat up. I had hoped to validate my worth by having someone pretend to care about me. It didn't work. I knew it right away.

I felt just awful afterward, terribly ashamed of my own actions. Desperate to square accounts with my faith, I confessed to the bishop of the church shortly thereafter. As a result, there was some brief talk of me being "disfellowed," but that never occurred. Instead, the hierarchy decided to hand down the following punishment.

1. I had to tell my husband (whom I was in the process of divorcing) what I'd done.
2. I couldn't teach the young women in the church anymore (okay, that was fair).
3. I couldn't take the weekly sacrament, which was tantamount to a confession before the congregation.
4. I lost my "temple recommend" and couldn't go to the temple.
5. I had to read a book about sin/adultery and forgiveness.
6. I had to talk regularly with a strong woman in the church who would help guide me.

My penance was to last for one year. After that, my privileges might be reinstated.

I remember thinking at the time that the Jesus I thought I knew would have said to me, "My child, you're a mess. Come, take my hand, and follow me. I'll show you a better way." Instead, at the very moment when I needed to believe I had redeeming value, when I needed to feel loved and supported, I felt shunned, shamed, and unworthy. I recall that reading the book on adultery and forgiveness toward the end of the year made me feel even worse, as though I would *never* be able to redeem myself. I had been too bad.

I accepted the punishment; I didn't know what else to do. I behaved perfectly and paid a full tithe the entire year. I did everything they told me to do. When my year of chastisement ended, I met with the bishop, regained my privileges, and got my temple recommend back.

But I never returned to that church. I no longer feared their retribution, nor did I believe my year of penance was helpful. Following the rules of my own conscience and finding a loving Higher Guidance instead of a punishing one led me to a place where an institution's rules could not.

I have struggled tremendously with organized religion ever since this incident. To be fair, I was quite happy in that church early on. I *loved* the people. I loved the community and the atmosphere of protection that came from living in a similar manner as others and following comprehensive guidelines for happiness. I drew great comfort from that.

In many ways, it would have been much easier to stay in my safe religious box with the illusion of security through conformity than it was to open the box and look beyond for my individuality.

A church can serve as a wonderful support system, but it can also divide and detach us from ourselves, from others outside the religious community, and from our Higher Guidance if it (the church) functions as our God. It should not be misused as a tool to judge us, shame us, or strip us of our worth.

I've since learned that another person or an organization can never determine my value. It must come from my own knowledge that I am a child of God: because of that simple but extraordinary fact, I have intrinsic worth. No one will ever take that away from me again.

I share my experience with you in hopes that you won't be afraid to find what's real for you and your spiritual foundation. I consider that to be the most important part of my journey. Perhaps it will launch you on your spiritual journey as well.

Learn for Thyself

Out of all the religions in the world, what are the odds that yours is 100 percent correct in all of its precepts? I'm no oddsmaker, but it seems to me the chances of that happening are pretty slim. Yet how many people acknowledge that reality?

It's easy to discard, minimize, or find fault with other religions, spiritual practices, and philosophies when you know little about them, when you've always been told they're wrong, or when they seem so different. But had you been born in another country, you likely would have a significantly different belief system or religious practice.

I've often wondered if various religions are grouped together according to what resonates with people based on their geographic background, genetics, or particular circumstances, somewhat like certain foods grow specifically in certain locations or climates. Imagine how boring it would be if you were limited to eating only those local foods! Of course, I'm not saying the world works this way, but it gives you an idea of what it's like to consider things from a different angle.

Whether you belong to an organized religion or not, spirituality *must* come from within. No one person, institution, or thing can give it to you. You must learn for yourself so you can *know* for yourself.

? .. Can you admit that there might be other good stuff out there, if only you would try it?

Starting with a Blank Slate

I became willing to set aside any and all beliefs I had previously held in order to find the weak points in my spiritual foundation. I longed for a spiritual support system that would never leave me, one that would help me to better handle the chaos surrounding my son's addiction.

I began with a blank slate and gave myself permission to do away with everything I thought I believed; I would start over and reconstruct my spiritual foundation from the ground up. Honesty is critical in such an endeavor, but I'll admit I was terrified to really examine and let go of some of my deeply ingrained beliefs. As I mentioned previously, I thought bad things would start happening, I'd be further punished, and my life would fall apart—even more than it already had (though I wasn't sure it could get any worse). I knew I had to try something, *anything* different. I couldn't go on the way I was; it just wasn't working. I got no solace, relief, or guidance in my present state of mind, only constant worry and dread.

For a long time, I didn't know how I felt about much of anything. Earlier, I had seen a counselor who kept asking for my opinions and thoughts on various things. It drove me crazy! I didn't have any answers for her, yet she kept pressing me, saying that I *did* know how I felt. But honestly, I really didn't. I was numb to my own feelings, for I had given so much of myself away by hiding my true thoughts, questioning my own judgment and worth, and adopting others' ways of thinking as my own.

Eventually, I came up with a question that has helped me discover how I truly feel. I ask myself: "If nothing else mattered and I wouldn't be struck down by lightning or worried what anyone else thought, what or how would I really believe?" This simple approach gives me the freedom to mull things over in my mind without fear of repercussions or causing any harm to myself or others. I don't have to take action on any of the answers I come up with, but I *do* get a good sense of where I stand on the issue at hand.

It was during my yoga teacher training that I first learned to be open to other ways of thinking and believing. At first, I was quite resistant, as we typically are when learning something unfamiliar, but I continued to listen, learn, and be receptive to new information. After all, I thought to myself, I didn't have to believe it; I could always reject it if I wanted to. But heck, it wouldn't hurt me to learn something. It felt good to discover this newfound freedom of making the choice for myself. I had never done that before.

I embarked on a journey of reading and learning, evaluating and discarding, trusting and letting go. I read the Old Testament and the New Testament, studied the *Yoga Sutras* and the *Bhagavad Gita*, took Jewish Kabbalah classes, read books on Buddhist and Eastern religion (some by

Pema Chodron), and scoured plenty of books on addiction. My favorites include *A New Earth* by Eckhart Tolle; *Autobiography of a Yogi* by Paramahansa Yogananda; the *Bhagavad Gita, The Yoga Sutras,* and *The Upanishads* translated by Eknath Easwaran; *A Return to Love* by Marianne Williamson; *When Things Fall Apart* by Pema Chodron; and the "Big Book" of Alcoholics Anonymous. (See the "References and Recommended Readings" section at the end of this book for more suggestions.)

Some of the material I read was way past what I could understand, but it nonetheless helped me to open my mind and consider things from many different perspectives. Slowly and surely, I felt my spirituality developing—or should I say returning?

There are certain things I feel sure of and others I still have no clue about, but the important thing is that I remain open. I give myself the freedom to continually change and evolve, whatever that may entail. And I don't use my spirituality as an excuse for poor behavior, as some (typically religious) people might claim when someone dares to adopt different beliefs or go their own way.

Scholars and wise men and women of God can serve well as guides, but they shouldn't be made responsible for your own divine knowledge. You have your own path to follow, and you alone must seize the reins on your spiritual journey. As you will find along the way, your divinity is the most amazing thing about you!

Questions to Consider When Rethinking Your Spiritual and Religious Views

When going through the process of reexamining my spiritual and religious beliefs, I asked myself a host of questions, among them:

1. Do I need to call my divinity God? What, if anything, do I want to call it?

2. How big is my God—bigger than my imagination?

3. Is my Higher Guidance vast enough to love all living beings, regardless of affiliation, descent, sexual preference, and so forth? Or is there inherent inequality between people?

4. Who is allowed to judge another?

5. Is one sin greater than another?

6. Are we all sinners or just imperfect human beings? What's the difference?

7. If we're all sinners, why are people still judging?

8. Who or what am I allowing to assume the role of God in my life— my children, my partner, my job, my church (hierarchy), my mind, my distractions?

9. Do I only turn to God when I have problems—that is, do I see Him as a problem-solver God rather than as an infinite God who can guide and inspire me through all things?

10. Do I need a church intercessor to experience God, or can I experience God directly?

11. Do I need to be in a religious building or be part of a congregation to experience or learn of God?

12. Am I truly experiencing God—or am I just following rules?

13. Does God have a gender?

14. Does the hierarchy of a church need to be male?

15. Do I believe in heaven?

16. Do I believe that there is only one way to heaven?

17. Do I believe in hell?

18. Do I believe in hell because I'm afraid not to?

19. Where is hell? What is hell?

20. Where is heaven? Are there different levels, as I was taught in one church?

21. Is heaven a place where only limited or good souls go? Do I feel the need to earn my way into heaven?

22. What constitutes a good soul? Is there such a thing as a bad soul or just bad behavior?

23. Is God within me or are we separate?

24. Is my God judgmental or loving?

25. Could God be energy and light?

26. Could reincarnation be true, or am I willing to say that it might be possible?

27. Do I believe in karma?

28. Does supporting a group that is contrary to a church's doctrine make you less worthy (such as an LGBT rights organization, an opposing political party, or a women's rights group)?

29. Could all religions and philosophies have some truth to them? Can I learn about different deities (for example, Hindu gods, Christian saints, or the gods in Greek mythology) and notice similarities without feeling my faith is threatened?

30. Can I let go of any attachments to what I've been taught and put other philosophies on a fair and equal footing when I'm evaluating new information? Which longtime attachments am I hanging on to and why?

31. Do I have the courage to admit that I may not have all the answers but go forward with what I now believe (even if it's not much at first) versus what I've been taught?

32. Do I believe there is any merit in doing things in a prescribed way? Or does protocol matter, as in the following arenas:
   • Rules of prayer (how to do it)
      ◦ Specific wording
      ◦ Specific location and time
      ◦ Frequency and duration
   • Appropriate behavior
      ◦ Proper dress (modest, covering certain parts of the body)
      ◦ Consumption of alcohol and certain foods (such as pork, meats of all types, or meat on Fridays)
      ◦ Premarital sex, abortion, and nontraditional marriage
      ◦ Cursing

?.. Have you ever asked yourself any of these questions? Did any of them provoke fear? Did any lead to deeper thinking?

In addition to these questions, I also made a list with two columns:

Attributes of My Old God	Attributes of My New God
• Punishing	• Never wavering
• Hard to understand	• Loves me no matter what
• Not always accessible or available	• Loves others just as much
• Judgmental	• Simple
	• Available

? .. How would you believe differently if no one would be harmed and you wouldn't be judged? What would your two columns look like?

Accessing the Deep-Down Stuff

At first, it was extremely difficult to access feelings that I had long suppressed in an effort to avoid dealing with them. Contemplating the questions helped me to shake up some of my thinking patterns and to notice where I might be clinging to old beliefs instilled by other people. The questions also helped me understand how I might see things differently if I felt safe enough to acknowledge (if only to myself) some of my honest opinions.

I had to remind myself, over and over again, about that thought-provoking query I mentioned previously: "If nothing else mattered and I wouldn't be struck down by lightning or worried what anyone else thought, what or how would I really believe?" This process gave me a lot more clarity, although I didn't always have definitive answers for the thirty-plus questions listed previously.

Though the process allowed me to view things more clearly, I found it difficult to know what to do with the new information I'd acquired. It took a while to absorb it and to comprehend how the change in my beliefs would affect my life more broadly. I knew I could not go forward acting as if I was the same person I had been before—yet I wasn't quite sure what that meant.

My son also had been going through a spiritual growth process. He was attending AA meetings at the time and had been clean for about nine months—the longest period he'd ever been without drugs or alcohol since his addiction set in (although he suffered a subsequent relapse).

For the first time, I began to see my son's addiction as something separate from him personally—and separate from me as well. He was such a different person when the drugs were not controlling his mind and body, and so was I. It was then that I got my first glimpse of what things could be like when each of us took control of our lives, instead of both of us suffering together.

I continued to probe my thoughts regarding the list of religious questions as I took in more and more information. I wondered, for instance, could reincarnation really be true? I had never wanted to believe in reincarnation because, frankly, I didn't want to come back to this world given all the pain and heartache I'd already endured. It seemed far preferable to believe that life is a "one-and-done" experience—I could go to heaven and avoid hell altogether, with no more suffering in store. Yet the more I read and learned, the more I had to admit that reincarnation *could* be possible. I may never know for sure (at least not in this lifetime!), but that's okay. Admitting to other possibilities signified growth for me, a major step forward in my spiritual journey. I don't need to know all the answers: as far as I can tell, no one does. For most people, spirituality doesn't arrive in an instant. It may come in small pieces, or it may come in chunks. It develops over time as we gradually learn to place our trust in it. If you are willing to believe in something greater and if you can be totally honest, you will continue to strengthen your personal presence and divine foundation.

… I began to see my son's addiction as something separate from him personally—and separate from me as well. He was such a different person when the drugs were not controlling his mind and body, and so was I.

Meditation and the Divine Dump:
Accessing Your Spiritual Power

One of the greatest tools for achieving self-knowledge is meditation. The concept of meditation gets thrown around a lot these days, especially in the yoga world, but it is rightfully gaining more universal acceptance thanks to its proven effectiveness.

I never understood how sitting alone and still, with your eyes closed and your mouth silently chanting some sort of gibberish, could make the slightest difference—until I tried it. Before then, I had never slowed down long enough to sit quietly and observe my breathing or trace my thoughts. I had been too busy reacting to life. But I would soon learn that establishing a regular meditation practice is an incredibly powerful and life-changing act. This is why.

There is power in your breath. A saying in the yoga world explains it this way: "As the breath, so the mind." Thus, when your breathing is rapid and shallow, your thoughts are rapid and shallow. By controlling the breath and slowing it down, you also control the mind chatter by slowing it as well. There's actually a term for these fluctuations of the mind, or mind chatter, among yoga practitioners—it's called *citta vritti*.

People in many diverse cultures across the globe find solace in meditation because it slows the chatter in the mind and allows peace, clarity, and discernment to enter in and replace the restless citta vritti. Without that tranquility, you cannot see situations and yourself clearly; filters such as fear, anger, and resentment distort your perceptions and assessments. Your ego tells you that you need to be better: you don't have enough, you don't do enough, and you will never *be* enough.

Through meditation, these distortions from the ego lose their grip on you. A quiet mind allows for an inward, personal connection with your truest self and your Higher Guidance. It provides deep insight regarding how you respond to and move in the world. Otherwise, you operate from a place where your restless ego constantly comes into contact with other restless egos; no one gets past the superficial realm that is ruled by fears and insecurities.

When the chatter slows down—even for a second—it creates an open space before the next thought begins. Within that space, the thinking mind rests, and you are receptive to divine knowledge or what I refer to as "the divine dump." In this pause between thoughts, you gain insight and wisdom from the deeper soul. Thereafter, you are better equipped to act from a place of clarity instead of being hampered by the fear filters that the ego imposes.

Meditation transcends the ego and gives you information about who you are and how you feel. It helps you recognize and connect with the goodness that already exists within you, and it allows you to rest for a while.

·{MY STORY}·

During the writing of this book, I had to deal with a number of troubling life events, and at times, I let that affect my meditation practice. I learned a good lesson in the process, though. If my meditation wasn't consistent or long enough to calm my mind, I'd become fearful. Everything would look scary, and calm seemed impossible to attain. But when I meditated on a regular basis, I felt centered and focused. I was able to stay on my path, writing the book; I did not react to external issues out of fear and switch direction. Even without perfect knowledge of how to proceed, I was able to take one step and then another, always moving forward. I realized that if I got ahead of myself by thinking about the future or planning too much, the fear would come back. Meditating helped me to stay present in the day I was in and concentrate on what I could accomplish at that moment, not in the days or weeks ahead.

Staying in the present is a great tool for dealing with your loved one's addiction. It helps you overcome your tendency to imagine terrible outcomes, which then fill you with fear. Slowing your mind down also helps you to deal with any current issues in a more rational and calm manner, while also reminding you of the depth and strength of your very being when you are not fearful.

Please take a look at the simple meditation exercise described in chapter 9. With it, you can start your own meditation practice—and that may well change your life!

The God of Your Own Reasoning

A huge light bulb moment for me came when I first read the following excerpt about faith and reason in AA's famous "Big Book." It shook me to my core and forever changed my life:

"Without knowing it, had we not been brought to where we stood by a certain kind of faith? For did we not believe in our own reasoning? Did we not have confidence in our ability to think? What was that but a sort of faith? Yes, we had been faithful, abjectly faithful to the God of Reason. So, in one way or another, we discovered that faith had been involved all the time!

"We found, too, that we had been worshippers. What a state of mental goose-flesh that used to bring on! Had we not variously worshipped people, sentiment, things, money, and ourselves? And then, with better motive, had we not worshipfully beheld the sunset, the sea, or a flower? Who of us had not loved something or somebody? How much did these feelings, these loves, these worships have to do with pure reason? Little or nothing, we saw at last."

©*Alcoholics Anonymous* 4th Edition, pages 53–54 are reprinted with permission of A.A. World Services, Inc. Please note, A.A. is a spiritual program, not a religious program.

What I took from the reading was this: I had indeed been believing in God the entire time, but the God that I was clinging to, the one who had failed me, was the "God of my own reasoning." It was painfully obvious to me that my own reasoning was limited, and as a result, it couldn't support me. It most definitely had failed me in tackling my son's addiction. Even at its best and most creative, my mind could not win that war.

It made sense to me that if I only believed in the God of my own reasoning, I would be basing my worth and the worth of others simply on our respective intellectual, logical interpretive ability. Yet certainly there had been times—as I watched waves roll endlessly across the ocean or as I first took my newborn child in my arms—when I felt the presence of a force much greater than my own chattering mind.

It occurred to me that a belief in the God of our own reasoning would also foster a sense of separateness; those with greater reasoning skills would be considered superior, whereas those with more modest skills would be deemed less worthy. That didn't make sense to me. Moreover, what a harsh and frightening way it was to view the world! If everyone was greater than or less than, how could we ever experience equality as children of God? It's no wonder we feel insecure so much of the time if that's how we understand the workings of the world.

To take the logic further, why couldn't I judge myself and others based on attributes such as athleticism or beauty, rather than on our inherent worth as human beings? Clearly, this way of thinking would be highly discriminatory and would serve to keep us living in fear, competition, and self-doubt. Sadly, this appears to be the way many Americans think.

·{ M Y   S T O R Y }·

When I first became a yoga teacher, I invited some friends and neighbors to my house so I could practice what I'd learned. One of the ladies I asked was a little hesitant. She was a devout Christian and asked if we would be saying "Aum" (or "Om") during the practice. She was quite uncomfortable with that.

Oddly enough, I understood where she was coming from. When I first heard people chanting "Aum" or "Om" at my teacher training, it freaked me out! I thought it was a weird thing to do, and I wasn't anxious to participate initially. I asked what the chant meant because I wanted to be sure I wasn't speaking some foreign language and inviting evil spirits in. So I can understand why people find the chanting strange. But I've since learned that strange things just might expand our world.

Remaining Open

Things that we don't know anything about always strike us as strange. Say you're offered a new food from some far-off location. You've never tasted it or seen anything like it before; you might not even be able to pronounce or spell its name. So it just seems weird. But that doesn't automatically mean it tastes bad or that it's something you should stay away from. It's just different—but only to us. Somewhere else on the globe, people have grown up with it and consider it as common as an apple.

By the way, many describe "Aum" (or "Om") as the universal sound of creation. It is formed by enunciating three different letters (A, U, and M), which produce different vibrations in the body as the sound moves from the belly and up through the chest, ending with the lips closed.

Sound vibration is a major deal in the yoga world and in sound therapy. I no longer think the chanted "Aum" is weird at all—in fact, I think it's really cool. An unbelievable, powerful energy emerges when a class of yoga students fully engages in the chant, blending separate voices to produce one harmonious, lovely sound.

Remember that it's always good to keep an open mind. Rejecting or excluding new ideas, experiences, and so forth because they are unusual or unfamiliar often stems from fear, and in the end, that can limit you and cause you to miss out on some truly amazing things.

Changing Your Beliefs and the Resulting Judgment of Others

·{ MY STORY }·

About four years after my divorce, I remarried. My new husband was a strong Christian. I had been raised as a Christian, although my family never attended services regularly. As I mentioned, I had left the church that punished me a few years earlier.

My new husband and I began attending a nearby Christian church, the one that allowed alcohol. The music was fantastic and the pastor captivating and humorous. Although the church had a few principles I disagreed with, I could usually count on feeling less burdened when I left a service or event there. And my involvement with this church only took about two hours out of my week; I didn't do much other than show up on Sundays (and I didn't even have to dress up for that). All in all, it seemed a nice fit, at least for a while.

I thought if I sat in the pew each week, listened to the pastor's message, and sang the songs, that would be enough. It never dawned on me that religion could be so much more than that.

Gradually, I realized that although I was connected with the church, my connection with God never grew any stronger. I was still stuck in fear most of the time, and my self-worth continued to suffer.

I had already begun to question religious things by that point but not wholeheartedly. During that period, my younger son was out of state trying to get or stay clean, my older son was away at college, and I was in yoga teacher training. My efforts to rethink my religion intensified, and shortly thereafter, my thinking turned into action.

It became clear to me that I didn't want to attend church on Sundays anymore. Something about it just didn't sit right with me, and I certainly wasn't getting any closer to God: I truly felt I was just checking the boxes and checking out. As the divide between what I believed and the underlying principles of the church widened, it actually felt dishonest for me to be there. But I didn't know how to break the news to my husband—or what might happen as a result.

It was difficult and even scary to discuss my feelings with my devoutly Christian spouse. After all, he was a preacher's son and had been a missionary kid. I didn't really know how to explain what was going on with me; in truth, I wasn't too sure about much of anything at that time in my life.

He was extremely troubled by the fact that I didn't want to go to church anymore and upset because I had said I was a Christian when we got married. He was right about that, and I felt badly. Yet I also knew I needed to grow. I had to take the risk. I wanted so much more, at a spiritual level, than what I currently had.

My husband never questioned his faith, and I was a little envious of him: I wanted that kind of certainty for myself too. And I knew that meant I needed to take control of my own spiritual progress and follow my own path.

Initially, I stopped going to church as regularly as before, and then I stopped going altogether. I was a little guilty at first, but things began to feel better and better over time. Meanwhile, I continued to study and read about spirituality and participate in other philosophies and practices, gathering a fascinating array of perspectives.

Though I didn't know exactly how or what I believed, I knew that I couldn't be dishonest with others or myself anymore. That's an okay place to be for a while, until you feel your own truth beginning to form. I realized that if I continued to attend church because another person expected me to, I would remain stuck in a box of someone else's beliefs. I could no longer live vicariously through another's faith.

I also came to understand that I had often denied my feelings during previous relationships. I had willingly put off any career plans to stay home with my children, and later on, I had neglected myself while trying to help my son overcome his addiction. Now, I knew that I no longer wanted to deny my emotions. I had given up so much of myself in the past, but I wasn't willing to do that in the future. It was high time I figured out what was real for me.

Over time, my husband began to see that I hadn't turned into some crazy person; instead, I was gaining insight into myself and becoming even more committed to loving and sharing with my fellow humans. I was happier. I came alive. I felt my worth for the first time as my connection with God began to form and grow. I think it made him understand that he might have been just a little judgmental when I first turned away from the church, perhaps because of his own fears.

Today, I remain open to new information and viewpoints as my own understanding of God, or universal energy, grows within me. I do not get upset that others have different perspectives. In fact, I'm grateful that we don't all have to adopt the same ideas and attitudes. In some ways, it's like my reaction to a crying baby at a restaurant or on a plane: I don't get upset that the child is howling because it isn't mine! I'm thankful that I have my own peace.

Maybe someday I'll attend a church again. Right now, though, it feels too limiting. I think a church can help you maintain your connection to God, but I don't think it can *establish* that connection for you. That requires action on your part. And that's where I find myself today.

Changing the Judgment Mentality

The judgment mentality that some people, religious institutions, and organized groups embrace can be downright terrifying. To them, I would pose the following questions: (1) Why can't the judgment of others be left up to God? and (2) If anyone's behavior is contrary to whatever you believe to be God's word, why can't God mete out the condemnation and punishment, if any is required? It appears to me that when the judging is left to God, life gets a whole lot easier for everyone. We're off the hook: we don't have to judge other people, and we don't run the risk of *mis*judging them either, which we are prone to do.

If you strongly identify with something outside yourself, be it a political party, a religion, a cause, or a specific point of view (for instance, that addiction is a disease and not a choice), you may be inclined to immerse yourself in that group or perspective. But if you become too deeply involved, you could end up living in duality or find that you're constantly playing a game of one-upmanship with others. You may be quick to judge people who do things differently or have other allegiances, certain that you are right and they are wrong. This behavior leads to separateness, disconnection, and divisiveness between individuals as well as their respective affiliations or causes. Such schisms lie at the heart of many arguments, deep resentments, and even wars between nations.

Perhaps another person's misunderstanding of your loved one's addiction-related behavior has hurt you badly. You know firsthand how damaging judgment can be. How often have you altered your words, hidden your pain, or withheld information regarding your situation in order to avoid being ridiculed or criticized? Having been in this position, you have empathy for those in unfortunate and uncomfortable circumstances.

True spirituality creates personal freedom instead of confinement. It contradicts judgment and allows you to see everyone as children of God, all of whom are inherently equal. Once you've accessed your own feelings, it becomes far easier to respect the feelings of others. This awareness also decreases your need to convert others to your point of view. After all, your opinions and feelings only need to work for you. As you give yourself permission to expand into your divine nature— rethinking and changing worn-out and borrowed perspectives—you extend that permission and freedom to others as well. You no longer need to draw a line in the sand, establishing that someone is right and someone else is wrong. Your sense of disconnection evaporates as you accept the fact that people simply think and feel differently. It's not you versus me, it's us.

> *True spirituality creates personal freedom instead of confinement.*

None of us has all the right answers. And none of us lives without pain and struggle. So what do you have to lose by seeking a Higher Guidance to help you navigate through life? Nothing. If you find that it helps you tackle the difficulties of daily life, then how can you err in choosing that path?

I have witnessed so many people transformed by finding their Higher Guidance, myself included, that I cannot dismiss its potential in anyone's life. When people experience God, they become aware of their value and view life in a totally different manner. As it says in the "Big Book" by AA, "When, therefore, we were approached by those in whom the problem had been solved, there was nothing left for us but to pick up the simple kit of spiritual tools laid at our feet. We have found much of heaven and we have been rocketed into a fourth dimension of existence of which we had not even dreamed."

What Does Spiritual Peace Feel Like?

Some people like the thrill of a chaotic, fast-paced life. It's the American way of doing things. It gives you a bit of an adrenaline rush and in a strange way makes you feel productive and alive: you are doing something, and it seems like progress.

However, if you love an addict, you know all too well that trying to control the impact of their crises and their disruptive behaviors is neither thrilling nor progressive. There are no perfect outcomes in addiction—or in life—so striving for perfection will only bring you added misery.

Continual effort results in busyness, not progress. By the same token, perfectionism impedes progress, and worse yet, it prevents peace of mind. It reinforces a cycle of endless striving and then falling short. (At the time of writing this particular section, my continual effort kept me rewriting for so long that I thought you might never get to read this!)

Finding a Higher Guidance that you can trust—even if just a little bit at first—allows you to let go of some of the controlling impulses that result from dealing with the repercussions of addiction—or simply from managing life in general. The saying "Let go and let God" reverberates because that advice works. It helps relieve you of the unnecessary burden of perfect outcomes.

When you decide to release your grip on life and accept that you don't have to bear the responsibility for everything turning out perfectly, the relief is immense. Amazingly, you begin to experience peace.

When you first encounter peace, it may feel strange. At least it did for me. I kept thinking I needed to drink some coffee or manufacture some pressure, drama, or deadline to speed things up again. I wasn't used to the calmness I now experienced; it was foreign to me. When I wasn't "doing" something, I felt uneasy at first, but strangely enough, my world did not fall apart—quite the opposite. Everything got much easier, and I got better.

Over time, the peace begins to feel more normal than the chaos. As you adjust to this new reality, you find you feel much better living with serenity. Life starts to slow down, and you have time to enjoy simple moments filled with gratitude, moments you never appreciated before when you were racing past and shoving them aside.

You grow more comfortable about not having the answers to all the world's problems—or even your own. You don't feel compelled to push an agenda. When you do act, you act from a place of stillness, which brings more clarity and discernment to all your actions and decisions. The more you lean into your Higher Guidance, the more you learn to rely on it for your tranquility, instead of worshipping the false god of perfectionism.

When you feel you could've handled a certain situation in a better manner, you don't berate or undermine yourself. Instead, you grant yourself some grace and use what you've learned to cope with things differently—not perfectly—the next time around.

There are no perfect outcomes in addiction—or in life—so striving for perfection will only bring you added misery.

The Ego Versus the Soul: Who's in Control?

The ego has a critical role in protecting you from harm. It elicits the reflex of fear and invokes the "fight-or-flight" response. Most people don't need to live with their fight-or-flight response continually engaged. But you, like many readers of this book, may well find it quite common to do so. You fear the enemy that is your loved one's addiction, and you are constantly on guard to ward off another attack.

The ego is mainly interested in self-preservation. It doesn't care about your peace of mind or your fellow man. It breeds competition and wants to win at all costs.

The ego dies when you die. But it doesn't want to die, so it will do everything it can to keep itself at the forefront of your mind and your endeavors. It needs to be needed. It is the chatter in your mind that blocks out peace and serenity. It is a breeding ground for fear. It will tell you that you're not worthy of good things, of self-love, or of love from others. And it will do its best to convince you that any changes you attempt in order to better yourself will surely fail.

·{ MY STORY }·

Deep down, I knew what I *should* do, what I *needed* to do with respect to my first marriage and the decision to divorce. But I got stuck listening to the scary, recurring messages playing in my head (courtesy of my ego) telling me I would fail on my own and reminding me of all the things I was going to lose and how much it would hurt my children. Other messages tried to rationalize my situation, arguing that I should be more grateful for all I had or that things really weren't so bad after all.

In those days, I had only a small amount of faith in anything greater than myself. As a result, I had nothing to count on or trust in to help me get through the rough times I was facing. I did not know how to interpret my fears or judge whether they were truly valid, and I certainly had no clue about dealing with them. I was just an anxious, nervous mess on a daily basis, similar to how I felt when I first became aware of my son's addiction.

I have since learned that the major sign telling me I'm reacting from my ego (instead of from my Higher Guidance) is fear. And for me, that usually manifests in the form of anxiety and restlessness.

We typically think of someone who's got a big ego as being arrogant or full of him- or herself. But when I'm in my ego, I'm scared out of my mind. Period. Everything frightens me—big things, little things, anything at all. That's my clue that I'm in the wrong mind space. It's only when I'm able to quiet my mind through some form of mindfulness practice (such as meditation, prayer, yoga, an Al-Anon meeting, or a spiritual or creative activity) that some peace returns. I can then trust that even if I don't know what the future holds, I *will* be all right—though I have no idea how.

Sometimes, we can't imagine how everything will ever work out or get done. There are so many moving parts involved in almost every situation we confront—and precious few guaranteed outcomes. Making the decision to change how we deal with the uncertainties of life is the most important step we can take—and then it always seems we are faced with a thousand other choices, just to see if we're serious!

Taking in all the uncertainties at once can be overwhelming. What I have learned is that things all get worked out in their own time. But we need to accept that they won't necessarily fall into place immediately or in the way we might've hoped or expected.

When things don't work out as we'd like, we may feel a huge amount of sadness, especially if we suffer significant losses in the process. Yet that doesn't mean things will always turn out badly or that we can never move on. In fact, things often turn out better than we could have imagined.

If the changes and losses we experience are big enough and painful enough, we eventually develop a new normal, which might include new people, a new location, or new endeavors. And with that new normal comes a real opportunity to find more meaning in our lives and a peace of mind that will grow with time and expand into most of the empty spaces inside us.

Letting Go of Your Greatest Fears

I've found that living with fear is usually much worse than confronting it head on. My greatest fear, which was my constant companion for the longest time, was that my youngest son would die or end up in prison as a result of his addiction.

·{MY STORY}·

I remember a time when my current husband's father, a retired missionary and pastor, came for a visit. He is one of those people who seem able to look right through you and instantly sense what is going on, which is always a little unsettling for me. During that particular visit, he told me that I hadn't let go of my son, and he pointed out that my own happiness still depended on the choices my son made. I said nothing in response, but inwardly, I got angry, thinking he was way off base in commenting on my child's situation and the way I was handling it. After all, I *had* let my son go. Obviously, the man didn't know what he was talking about!

My father-in-law then suggested that instead of praying for specific circumstances to change, perhaps I should pray for my son to find his own Higher Guidance. Then all the other pieces would fall into place.

When I got past my self-righteous indignation, I began to feel uneasy—my clue that something else was going on with me. His comments reverberated in my troubled mind for a few days before I realized the truth: "Darn it," I admitted to myself, "he is right."

I thought I had let my son go, but I really hadn't. In a prayer to my Higher Guidance, I gave Him my son. I prayed that He would take care of him and heal him so he'd have a better life. In reality, though, what I had done was give my son to God *conditionally*. I gave him to God so that God could do what I wanted for my son.

I realized I had to give my son to God without condition. That prayer was the hardest one I've ever said and was accompanied by the shedding of many tears. It went something like this: *"God, I give you my son completely. I give you my greatest fears surrounding my son; I'm so afraid that he will die or go to prison and I don't think I could handle either one. Though I don't want those things to happen, I trust that You know what's best for him. I trust that You're with him as You are with me. I trust that whatever happens, I will be okay, even though I don't know how."*

As hard as it was to deliver that prayer, it brought me great peace. It freed me to move forward with my own life and not be so enmeshed in my son's. Some people could never say a prayer like that. And the truth is, I wouldn't have been able to say it either until my trust in a Higher Guidance became stronger than my fear.

When I pray these days, it's much easier. I don't have to obsess about including all the right details or asking for all the things I think are necessary for my son to be healthy and happy. Heck, I don't have all the right answers or know the best path for myself, let alone anyone else. So now I pray that both of my sons find their Higher Guidance. That would be the greatest thing that could happen to them. It's a simple yet powerful prayer.

Facing Your Fears

You get to decide on a daily basis whether you want to face your fears or deny them. Keep in mind that with each fear you confront, your personal power increases. Moreover, once you challenge a fear, it begins to lose its ability to control your life. Before long, the very thing you fear the most turns into strength as you meet it head on and move through it instead of being anchored to it.

That is not to say that you will never get scared again. You will. You cannot avoid all fears—indeed, some are critical to survival. But when you find yourself stuck in fear, here are three strategies that will help you pull yourself up and out of the anxiousness and paralysis that fear often creates.

- **Accept the present.** Look the uncertainty in the eye and acknowledge it, without trying to change it.
- **Trust in the process.** Trust your Higher Guidance to guide you through the fear instead of using self-will to force a solution.
- **Detach from the outcome.** Let go of what might happen. Live in gratitude that your greatest fear often isn't real *right now* (it typically exists only in your mind at that moment).

?..Have you given your greatest fear to your Higher Guidance? Are you living your life in fear or freedom?

Signs Your Life Is Beginning to Shift

Because of your willingness to rethink and reevaluate your past beliefs and come to terms with any that no longer serve you, a fresh spiritual connection can be formed. This connection allows a whole new world to open up, one in which any deception or prejudiced thinking is brought into plain view and set aside so a better life can emerge. Following are some of the signs that indicate a transformation is under way:

- Your Higher Guidance dictates your composure more often than your loved one's behavior.
- You rest in the security of your worth. You won't care about being

judged, for you're secure in who you are and what you believe, even if you don't know exactly where you (and your loved one) are headed or how you'll get there.

- You accept other people's choices. Just as you are afforded the right to have and live your own beliefs, you grant that same right to others. You don't need to justify or judge because you don't feel threatened in any way.
- Life begins to flow. You've stopped fighting and resisting life. Circumstances and people "come out of nowhere" to help you (and your loved one) on your path. Change happens without you forcing it.
- You experience truthful expression. You may find yourself making major changes as you begin to rethink other areas of your life in which you feel misrepresented or at odds, such as in a marriage or career. You may take up new hobbies and find new friends in unexpected places as you explore new interests and lifestyle changes.
- You experience serenity. You begin to realize that chaotic living is antithetical to peace. You know what peace feels like and desire more of it.
- You gain insight and recognize when you feel uneasy, fearful, or out of sorts. You interpret these feelings as clues alerting you that something is amiss or that you've strayed from your spiritual path. You learn to relax your grip on things again, and you find your way back more quickly to your Higher Guidance or place of peace.
- You feel worthy of self-love. You start taking better care of yourself, both physically and mentally—for instance, by adopting new eating patterns, taking up yoga, meditating, or pursuing creative endeavors that rejuvenate your spirit and light up your personality.
- Your actions and behaviors come from strength, not weakness. You find new courage to establish boundaries that limit and prevent unacceptable behavior and harm by others.
- You garner respect. Even your addicted loved one will regard you differently, although they'll hate your changes at first. For them, those changes mean they cannot treat you the way they have in the past. If they want to continue their relationship with you, they will have to alter their behavior. You become a great model for them, showing how to change one's life for the better.
- There is no reason to settle anymore. You resolve to make the most of your life and fill it with more joy than misery.

6

The 3 Rs for the Soul: The Second R — Reclaiming Your Personal Power

Controlling What You Can

You have the power to control many things in your life. You can, for instance, decide to set your alarm clock earlier tomorrow so you'll have time to meditate. Or you can choose what foods you will put into your mouth, determine what color of clothing you'll wear, or opt to exercise or not.

By and large, however, many aspects of life are totally beyond your control. You have no power to affect the choices an adult family member makes, nor can you fight your loved one's battle with addiction. You can't prevent being laid off in a corporate downsizing, nor can you plan a serendipitous meeting that leads to your next job. A host of random events will shape your life, for good or ill—a chance encounter with your future spouse, a car accident, an illness. And clearly, you have no influence on your genetic makeup or the time and place of your eventual demise. You do your best to avoid the unpleasant stuff, but you cannot always prevent it. Consequently, you can't help but live with a degree of apprehension about life's uncertainties and the twists and turns of fate.

Somewhere between the things you control and the things you do not is a large gray area—a place where you *think* you can affect outcomes such as another person's behavior. The trouble is, no matter how fervently you believe you have that power, you simply don't. Many people spend a lot of time in this gray area. Sadly, they are wasting precious time and energy when they do so, and no doubt they bring much frustration and pain into their own lives in the process.

You don't always know what's best for others or even for yourself. How many times have you been sure that you had the answer to a problem only to have something unexpected happen that brings a totally different—and often better—result?

Mortal knowledge is limited, of course. It's easy to think you know best in certain situations (especially if you're a parent or used to being in charge). It seems obvious, for example, that an alcoholic or addict should go to rehab and stop drinking or drugging, right? But you don't have the power necessary to precipitate that or any other change in them unless they are on board. They need to do for themselves, just as you do for yourself.

When you use your personal power in a forceful manner to try to stop things from being the way they are (or turning out the way you fear), you make yourself miserable and drive those around you crazy—and you're likely to fail anyway. I understand the impulse to do anything and everything possible to save a loved one who's in danger. But in the end, it's extremely difficult, if not impossible, to save someone who doesn't wish to be saved. And you often lose yourself along the way.

Although it sounds contradictory, accepting some amount of powerlessness actually is quite a powerful move. Differentiating between what you can control and what you cannot is one of the biggest keys to preserving your emotional health and reclaiming your personal power.

A breakthrough occurs—and a huge weight is lifted off your shoulders—when you begin to understand this difference and realize that you don't need to control as much as you thought you did. I like this definition—*Powerless: no ability to make right something that is wrong, or something that you don't like.*

Feeling powerless is not failing, and it's not being weak. It is simply acknowledging that you do not have the ability to control everything. In reality, letting go of the things you can't control (and leaving them to a Higher Guidance) is acting from a place of strength and wisdom.

You may experience the feelings of vulnerability and helplessness that often accompany letting go of control, until you understand that the true power *comes* from letting go. After all, you never really had control to begin with—that was just an illusion. Now you can see that you no longer need to create an agenda to make things right. Set that burden aside.

Two Types of Power: Productive and Destructive

1. **Productive power—a good use of your power.** This includes, among other things, maintaining boundaries (see chapter 8), accepting responsibility as opposed to blaming others, trusting in a Higher Guidance, trusting yourself, and effecting personal change.

    This type of power is more in alignment with your natural, spiritual self. It helps you reclaim the pieces of yourself that you have given to people and situations, by setting boundaries and changing negative patterns. Productive power leaves you feeling far more complete and balanced. It derives from a deeper knowledge of who you really are—a worthwhile human being—and what you stand for. It fills you with intentions of humbleness and forgiveness and gives you clarity and love to contribute to the greater good as well as to yourself. It embraces a reverence for something much larger than you, and it shapes all decisions you make.

2. **Destructive power—a misuse of your power.** This includes, but is not limited to, trying to manipulate, coerce, and control people and situations; retaliating against others; judging or suppressing others; and using bullying, narcissistic, or abusive behaviors. Controlling behavior is an arrangement you create to give yourself the illusion of certainty.

Using this type of power to save your loved one from their choices drives you crazy. You get caught up in the illusion that *you*, not they, must do something in order for everything to be okay. You wield your best-loved tools—guilt, anger, shame, self-righteousness, and fear—to get your way. This unhealthy pattern never changes until *you* change how you react to the people and events that affect your life. Until then, your controlling tendencies are a misuse of power. Eventually, they wind up controlling you.

Once you have begun establishing a strong and engaged spiritual foundation for yourself, you will be ready to continue on your journey of self-reflection—a journey that will lead to your becoming the world's foremost expert on your life. Along the way, you will reclaim your personal power. Imagine being the person you know the most, love the most, and trust the most—as much as you know, love, and trust your Higher Guidance!

In the pages ahead, I discuss five specific steps you can take to build productive power. I urge you to incorporate them into your life. You'll find that, in fairly short order, they'll produce some amazing results that will help you simplify your life and reconnect with your natural potential. As you examine these approaches, you're liable to recognize patterns and behaviors that have impeded your progress in the past. Now you can rethink them and find a better way. You can remove these self-imposed obstacles and clear the path that lies before you. Once you stop fighting yourself, you'll be ready to start embracing life.

Differentiating between what you can control and what you cannot is one of the biggest keys to preserving your emotional health and reclaiming your personal power.

Five Keys to Creating Productive Power

1. NEVER, EVER LIE TO YOURSELF

The number one way in which you can expand your personal power and change your life for the better is by being honest with yourself. Without honesty, you will live a contrived life, remaining stuck in your junk and wondering why you never get where you want to go. You've already done some of the work when rethinking your spiritual base. You had to be honest and sincere as you questioned how you truly felt about your deeply held beliefs.

You probably consider yourself a truthful person. You don't overtly lie to others in the context of your daily life, you don't steal from others, you try to be genuine in your communications, and you hold up your end of an agreement if you give your word.

Yet there are many other ways to be insincere, ways you don't always consider when assessing your honesty. This is particularly true in regard to feelings surrounding intensely personal matters—information you don't wish to share with others, for to do so would shine a light on your supposed defects and cause others to judge you just as harshly as you've already judged yourself. Examples of such matters include being a victim of rape, incest, abuse, or a cheating spouse, or a failure of any kind. The self-deception arises when you wrongly interpret these occurrences as detrimental to your intrinsic value. You may have been harmed or felt like you failed, but your underlying worth remains intact.

It's possible that you are unaware of engaging in a specific obstacle-producing behavior until someone points that out to you or circumstances make it clear. If this occurs, you have to be honest enough to admit that what you've learned may actually be true.

·{ MY STORY }·

I'll never forget the day my divorce attorney walked me to my car after a particularly hostile meeting with my soon-to-be former spouse and his attorney. When we reached my car, she told me that what she had just witnessed was classic, textbook emotional abuse. I was shocked! I didn't want to believe it. I did *not* want to be a weak, emotionally abused woman. It didn't fit with who I thought I was or who I wanted to be. At that moment, however, I knew that it was true. Other people had told me something similar, but this was the first time I got the message. Until then, I had always blocked the thought from my mind or hastily pushed it away. I could not go on denying it anymore. For the first time, I was honest with myself regarding this painful reality. But only by finally admitting it was I able to accept that aspect of my emotional tendencies and move forward to change it. In time, I came to understand that living with emotional abuse didn't mean I was unworthy. On the contrary, I just didn't fully comprehend my value. (For more on emotional abuse, see the article "I'd Rather Take a Hit" reprinted in Appendix B.)

We all tend to repress humiliations and harms we have suffered in the past as well as unhealthy dependencies. In extreme cases, we may have lived with a bad situation for so long that we don't even realize it's still lurking in the shadows. At some point, intense fear or pain compelled us to avoid these tough issues or stuff them away in an effort to protect ourselves from further harm. Then, because we have devalued ourselves in the process, we do everything we can to keep others from discovering our dark secrets and finding out who we really are. With practice, we may get so good at this deception that we even hide the truth from ourselves. Meanwhile, we live with the fear that we have lost the person we thought we were—or, worse still, become the person we never wanted to be.

Perhaps we didn't think any of this self-deception and repression mattered at the time, but eventually, we find that it does. These hidden nuggets of hurt and shame become impediments to our growth. In concealing them and masking our pain, we hide our very essence behind a wall of wasted energy and false security, denying it the opportunity to express itself in the world.

Acknowledging the not-so-pretty pieces of ourselves doesn't mean that we must parade them before the entire universe. But we *should* stop running from them and learn to accept them. We should stop hiding from ourselves. Otherwise, we will project a false image of ourselves into every situation we encounter and every relationship we pursue.

When we feel safe enough or when we have been hurt enough, we can begin a deep search of the self, acknowledging our painful and frightening experiences and thereby depriving them of the power to harm us further. We see that our experiences do not define us. Instead, we learn from them and grow with the knowledge we attain. We are who we are largely because of our experiences, but they cannot make us bad or dictate how we will behave in the future. As we gain wisdom and acknowledge our secrets, we can transform our pain. In fact, that pain might well become the catalyst that leads us to joy and rekindles some of the passion and purpose missing in our lives.

How can we expect to know what our purpose is and why we exist if we are always concealing who we truly are? How can we expect others to accept us if we can't accept ourselves?

At some point, we come to the realization that shining the light of day on the darker side of ourselves (or who we think we are) is liberating and affirming. Contrary to what we've long assumed, we learn that expressing ourselves as honestly as possible does not diminish our worth in any way; rather, it enhances our self-knowledge and self-acceptance. In that moment, we become free—free to be our true selves, in all our glory. Now, instead of spreading pain, we can spread love.

?
.. What painful truths have you buried in the deep, dark crevices of yourself?

One of the *best* things about speaking your truth is that you never need to defend or rationalize it. Instead, *your truth defends you.* It is what it is. Though others won't always like or support your truth, they can't argue with it or poke holes in it; they can only do that when you are hesitant, unsure, and indecisive or when you're telling them what you think they want to hear. Your truth is yours alone.

When you aren't secure in your truth, it seems flimsy and hard to defend because you waver in your own support of it. You put yourself in a weakened position and feel the need to substantiate or explain it because you inherently know it is flawed; you get lost in the myriad permutations and nuances surrounding it. Guess what? Others sense that insecurity and pounce on it when they are hurt or offended. But when you speak your truth with confidence and clarity, you never have to bolster it. It stands for itself.

When you are courageous enough to speak your truth, confrontation eventually decreases. Others might be disgruntled or hurt, but most people recognize truth when they hear it, and they usually know they can't change it. Over time, they must accept it even if they don't like it.

Two things are necessary for speaking one's truth. First, you must know what your truth is. Then, you must feel safe enough to express it.

Perhaps you have no idea what your truth is. As suggested earlier, you might have stuffed your feelings deep down inside yourself for so long that you've become numb and don't know how you really feel.

You suppress difficult feelings in order to protect yourself; you are afraid of what speaking up might mean. If you were belittled when you spoke up in the past, you might remain quiet to avoid any possible humiliation or retaliation. Of course, you pay a price. When you fail to express yourself, your unique voice is silenced.

Rediscovering your voice and giving yourself permission to speak usually takes time and occasionally distance as well. You may need to get away from a person or situation that paralyzes your ability to discern how you really feel. But even if recovering your voice happens slowly, I can assure you that you haven't lost your voice forever. Fear has merely silenced it temporarily. All your thoughts are still there to guide you, but only *you* can grant yourself permission to express them in speech—and that usually requires you to feel both free and safe.

Not all truths are big and earth-shattering. A lot of mine were small and even seemed silly, such as admitting I enjoyed watching a certain soap opera to my boyfriend (now husband). I wanted to present myself to him as an intelligent woman, and I worried he might think I was stupid if I watched the show, so I hid that little truth away and never turned the soap on when he was around. It's embarrassing to admit this now, but that's what I believed early on in our relationship. I was in fear, trying to be the kind of person I thought he would like instead of being myself. It seems ridiculous in retrospect, but it shows how easily we can get hung up on little untruths.

Here are three tools to use when you find yourself unsure and wish to clarify your truth:

1. **Try meditation and prayer:** Both activities are incredibly effective in reducing the constant chatter in your mind—you'll be amazed after you've incorporated these practices into your life for a while. When your mind is quiet, you can cut through the clutter of crazy thinking and access the core issue with brutal, often humbling honesty. You can then determine what is really going on in your head, what you're afraid of, and what you're so reluctant to admit, especially out loud. (See chapter 9 for a simple meditation practice.)

2. **Consider this clarifying question:** If, say, you weren't worried about anyone else's opinion, if no one would get hurt, or if money wasn't an issue, ask yourself, "If nothing else mattered, what would I do?" Maybe you'd do what I did (eventually): you'd watch the darned soap opera, get divorced, leave your church, wear rainbow pants, and be open about your loved one's addiction. This question helps clarify how you feel deep down.

3. **Consider a second clarifying question:** Now ask, "Am I rationalizing myself away from my own truth, as revealed in the first clarifying question?" Whenever you find yourself rationalizing, it means you're moving farther and farther away from your personal truth—that is, what you would do if nothing else mattered. For example, you're probably rationalizing when: you tell yourself the paint on the gorgeous red car might fade faster or be too flashy, so you should just get the white car; you decide the blue pants would be more practical even though the orange ones would be more fun to wear; you convince yourself that you get paid too much to leave the boring job you're in; or you keep telling yourself your loved one's addiction isn't really so bad—it's just that you're too critical.

Sometimes, you may decide that your rationalization is actually appropriate and reasonable, such as when your child's needs should prevail or when harm might ensue. But at other times, you aren't in a position, whether due to fear or circumstances, to act in accordance with your truth. Whether you act immediately or not doesn't always matter. What matters is that you recognize and acknowledge how you truly feel, rather than dismissing your feelings out of hand. Awareness of your truth is the first step. After that, you can take baby steps or giant leaps. It's up to you.

In the beginning, speaking your truth is so scary. You're not used to it, and it's terribly uncomfortable. It's like taking off the training wheels from your bike as a child—you feel wobbly and panicky as you pedal on. But the new freedom that comes with the realization that you're okay on your own is exhilarating! It might mean a few hair-raising rides and some bumps and bruises along the way, but it is a wonderfully liberating experience. The outcome validates your newfound freedom and gives you the courage to do it all over again in the future.

When you start speaking your truth, you may move from one end of the spectrum to the other—keeping your mouth shut and your thoughts in your head, on one extreme, and boldly shouting your absolute truth, on the other. When I was learning to speak my truth, I often got so emotional that I ended up yelling it to the person I was with; obviously, I had kept it captive for way too long. It takes practice to find that balance whereby you can speak truthfully yet also discern when being truthful might be harmful or when it won't benefit the situation (for instance, telling a drunk person you don't like it when they drink). You may swing past center when learning to articulate and vocalize your truth, but hang in there. With practice, you just may hit a home run.

Be prepared, though, for things to get worse before they get better. As a rule, people don't like change, so they resist it, sometimes furiously. Those closest to you will have the hardest time dealing with your new voice; they may criticize and demean you and generally make your life miserable for a while.

One of the things that happens when you are strong enough to speak your truth is that other people might not be secure enough to speak theirs or to handle yours. Therefore, it sometimes feels a bit isolating. Keep on speaking your truth.

Most people only like change when it comes on *their* terms. Your transformation means they will have to change how they interact with you, and they likely just won't want to do that. I have found one thing to be true, however, in matters like this. When you change for the better, it is often contagious, resulting in positive changes in those around you over time. When you modify the rules, others either adapt or keep their distance. As a result, you'll probably end up with better relationships based on mutual respect or else find yourself pulling back from relationships that were unhealthy in the first place. One of the things that happens when you are strong enough to speak your truth is that other people might not be secure enough to speak theirs or to handle yours. Therefore, it sometimes feels a bit isolating. Keep on speaking your truth.

Here are several areas in which you might find you're being dishonest with yourself. The behaviors described in the list that follows, even those that seem relatively insignificant, can actually give you great insight into where you may deviate from your own truth in order to project an image (of yourself, your family, your career, and so on) that is at odds with reality. This insight helps you understand how your behaviors may be keeping you stuck and unhappy because you are not addressing the underlying issues in your life.

Adopting Socially Accepted Excuses

• **Staying in the marriage for the kids.** Some people stay in a marriage because of fear but blame it on not wanting to harm the kids. Others say they can't break the solemn vows they made when they wed. Neither reason is bad or wrong. The vows we make *are* important, and it's natural to want to protect our children; I know my kids were my first priority. In all honesty, however, the sum total of my fears—about the reaction of family and friends, the uncertain financial implications, and the upheaval that a major lifestyle change might bring—was as great as my concern for my sons. I wasn't staying married just to protect my children; I also stayed because I was scared to death that I might not be able to make it on my own! So acting as if I was reluctant to get a divorce only because I wanted to protect the children would've been partially false. Remember, *none* of these kinds of fears or rationales are bad or wrong; it's just that you need to get clear about what you're really afraid of. Otherwise, you'll be lying to yourself and others.

• **Working too hard because your job is so important.** Are you devoting too much time and energy to your job at the expense of a balanced life? It's easy to inflate your self-importance by thinking you are irreplaceable and that your company "needs" you. Or maybe you're assuming your job title dictates your worth. Of course, there are legitimate reasons to work extra hard at times. You may have to put in a lot of hours to keep a position you like because the job market is tight or to get the experience required for the job you really want. But your job title does not define your worth. And don't kid yourself about being indispensable just because you're willing to work way more than everyone else: you can and one day will be replaced. *The bottom line is that you are not as important as you think because of what you do.* Working too much may also be an escape—an "acceptable" way to avoid dealing with an unhappy home life. If you're working all the time, be honest with yourself and get clear on the real reason behind this behavior. Are you avoiding some issue elsewhere in your life that needs to be addressed?

Always Giving In

• **Allowing another's views to trump your own.** Let's say you want to change your eating habits, drink less alcohol, do things differently on Saturdays, stop attending church on Sundays, or drop out of college, but you're not sure your partner or family will support you in the endeavor. If you don't make the change because of their potential resistance, you are choosing to dismiss your own preferences. *This avoidance can foster resentment within you—sometimes toward them but ultimately toward yourself.* In reality, it's the fear of trying to make the change alone, being made fun of, and possibly failing that stops you. It's frequently easier to remain quiet and accept the status quo rather than tackle the hard work of being honest with yourself and making the change. Oddly enough, it often wouldn't matter to the other people in the first place; they might even be grateful if you spoke up and asserted yourself. Naturally, you sometimes need to participate in things that might not be your top choice (to support your child or your partner, for example), but you don't always have to conform to other people's preferences. For example, when I was abstaining from alcohol, many times I gave in and went to events where everyone was drinking, so I did too. I would've preferred to be elsewhere, but I hadn't spoken up. As a result, I sometimes pouted (so mature!) or got angry and frustrated for putting myself in that position— and then everyone was unhappy. I've since learned that if I don't speak up, any resulting frustration is my own darn fault. I've also learned that the light-hearted rebellious thing to do is drink water or seltzer instead of alcohol. Who cares if everyone else is drinking liquor? The old saying "If you can't beat 'em, join 'em" doesn't need to apply anymore. Another approach I could take would be to say I don't wish to attend and then do something that's more to my liking. Either way, I'd be reclaiming my power over my choices and taking responsibility for my own happiness, as opposed to capitulating and being upset and resentful.

• **Settling for an uninspired sex/love life.** Maybe you're afraid to speak up about what you need or like in bed for fear of making yourself vulnerable and possibly being judged or rejected. Perhaps you may act like everything's fine; you're independent and don't need (or deserve) any specific affection or physical attention. But if you behave this way, you shut off the part of yourself that craves and needs love, and that will leave you an uptight, lonely mess. You may find yourself mired in unfulfilling patterns or habits in this regard. Sometimes, it can seem easier to sleep with a stranger and pretend to be the person you want to be rather than trusting that your partner will accept the person you are.

• **Disagreeing with others but remaining silent.** Have you ever disagreed with another's views on something you deem important yet remained silent? It is definitely easier to keep quiet, and in certain situations, it's prudent as well. You don't necessarily need to express your views when you know it will cause controversy or if you are dealing with someone who is unreasonable and argumentative. But discretion isn't always the better part of valor. You have a right to decide how and when you use your voice and what causes matter to you enough to warrant speaking up. For instance, if anyone around me expresses a negative view about gay people, it is hard for me to remain mute. I've found that if I speak up honestly, that usually puts a stop to further disparaging remarks, at least in my presence. And maybe, just maybe I've caused someone to at least question his or her own stance. I don't need to be mean or rude to be effective, of course, and just because I express my contrary opinion doesn't necessarily make me right and them wrong. I'm simply acknowledging that I have a different perspective and that I'm uncomfortable with the present conversation.

• **Accepting the unacceptable.** You should never allow others to treat you in a manner that is disrespectful or harmful. Should that happen, you need to voice your feelings and establish firm boundaries to protect yourself. (Read more about protective boundaries in chapter 8.) This problem happens a lot when you love an addict or alcoholic, for they become manipulative and untrustworthy in their addiction. Yet you often fall for their lies and deception hook, line, and sinker. It's hard to accept that someone you love would ever treat you so badly. You probably would never accept this behavior from anyone else, but because they're your loved one, you feel compelled to tolerate the intolerable—and be as miserable as they are. You may not even realize how far down the path of unacceptability you've traveled until your psychological and physical health suffer as a result. *The dishonesty in this situation stems from the fact that at some level, you actually believe you deserve to be treated this way.*

Manipulating the Way You Present Yourself to Others

• **Maintaining the perfect facade.** You never share your hurt, frustration, or sorrow with others, for fear of seeming less than perfect. To be sure, there is a place and time to be discreet, but to act as if your troubles don't exist, as if you're stronger than everyone else, and as if you have everything under control is being false. Perhaps you don't want people to know that you're struggling financially, that your partner is an alcoholic, or that your child just dropped out of high school. Why *would* you want others to see the shame you see in yourself as a result of these supposedly discreditable circumstances? Everyone has issues in life. In fact, it just might be that your problems are less severe than the next person's. Anyone who hasn't dealt with at least one serious personal problem is either unbelievably fortunate or too young to have experienced much of life yet. Always keep in mind that these types of troubles aren't at all indicative of your worth (though in our society, that's hard to accept, as the media constantly bombards us with portrayals of perfection). In reality, it takes a much stronger person to share pain and heartache rather than hide it. You don't have to broadcast your problems to the whole world, but by being honest and forthright when possible, you may find others who are in similar situations and realize that you're not alone in your suffering or brokenness.

Perhaps you can even soften the hard blows of life for another through sharing, caring, and offering support.

• **Trying to impress.** Have you ever met someone new or interviewed for a job and felt the need to impress the person across from you? (Daily, maybe?) Perhaps someone asks you on a date and wants to know what movie you'd like to watch, where you'd want to eat, or what you'd like to do the next weekend. How many times have you tailored your response in hopes of getting off to a good start? Because you don't want to appear selfish, needy, or bossy, you may try to pass yourself off as an easygoing, go-with-the-flow type of person, even if you're anything but. Or maybe a potential employer asks you what you most dislike about yourself or whether you're willing to travel and work extra hours to do what it takes to get the job done. If you really hate traveling and don't want to work around the clock, have you been up front about your preferences? Or have you given the impression that you'd love being on the road or working into the wee hours? It's not always easy to be honest, especially when you need the job. I remember interviewing with a Big 8 accounting firm toward the end of college. When the interviewer asked me what I most disliked about myself, I answered, "My thighs." I was being honest and open and attempting a bit of humor at the same time. I did not get hired.

Honesty is a hard-won virtue—indeed, being honest is one of the toughest things you do. Dishonesty, by contrast, is easy and often unrecognizable because of its subtleness. But only by being honest can you move forward into your life with purpose and conviction. When you make a resolute effort to give honesty a large place in your life, you are rewarded with a newfound freedom of personal expression and the pure joy that comes with acting from your core.

Next time, ask, "What's the worst that can happen?" Then push yourself a little further than you dare.

2. CREATING LESS PAIN

Many times, the harm we do to ourselves exceeds the harm others do to us. The following list describes common harmful behaviors that we engage in but that we can control once we realize they're at play in our lives. As you read through the pages ahead, consider how these behaviors diminish your personal power—and how you can make the necessary changes to replenish it. And remember that the less you harm yourself, the less you will spread harm to others.

Negative Self-Talk

As much as you fear being judged by the rest of the world, your fiercest critic lies within. Your harsh self-judgment and negative self-talk often conspire to undermine your best efforts and keep you stuck. The end result may be a battered version of yourself that is at odds with your divine nature.

Becoming a staunch self-supporter grows easier as you begin to realize and claim your worth and spiritual wholeness, following the first of the 3 Rs—"Rethinking Your Religious and Spiritual Beliefs"—as discussed earlier. You no longer feel the need to punish yourself for any perceived lack of worth because you've learned that's an illusion. You understand that your worth doesn't depend on perfection, and you stop striving for that unattainable goal.

You have a choice. On one hand, you can spend time demeaning and punishing yourself because you said or did something imperfectly or because you're disenchanted with a matter as big as life or as small as your looks. Or, on the other hand, you can use that same amount of time to enjoy your life and those around you.

Take one simple example: would you rather play in the ocean or stay in your hotel room because you don't feel comfortable in a swimsuit? You fear that everyone on the beach will judge your appearance—but all those judgy people are actually in your head! Everyone else is enjoying the water (or stuck in their own heads judging themselves)!

You can be your harshest critic or your greatest advocate. It's possible and much more fulfilling to play in the world around you instead of replaying old reels of negative self-talk in your mind. *Live in the world, not in your head.* It's a far more exciting place to be!

A strong spiritual connection and a quiet mind diminish ineffective thought patterns. They help you to create new, positive pathways in your brain instead of continually falling into the old, habitual ruts that you've defaulted to in the past.

The field of neuroplasticity has provided great evidence and inspiration in finding that changing the neural pathways in the brain is indeed possible and that the changes can persist for a lifetime. Practicing a new skill, such as meditation, and rethinking and modifying old habits help to encourage the formation of new pathways. It takes time and consistency to build these different connections, but it *is* possible. Certainly, it's worth the effort to embrace new approaches that aid you in building a healthier, more joyful existence.

… placing blame will neither change what happened nor prevent it from happening again.

Blaming Others: Giving Away Your Personal Power and the Problem with Always Being Right

I've come across many words of wisdom in the course of writing this book. On the topic of blaming others, I especially like the following thought: *when we feel that another person has hurt us unjustly, we can look back at our past decisionmaking to determine how we placed ourselves in a position to be harmed.*

This insight really resonates with me, for it highlights a critical way in which we give our personal power and happiness away, placing them, perhaps unwittingly, into the hands of others. If you look back, you can usually discover that you've played a role in the current dilemma all along.

When you feel wronged or when things don't go the way you want, it is quite natural to place the blame on someone else. It's much easier, of course, and it lets you off the hook for any consequences that follow. Your dilemma is clearly their fault. If only they hadn't done this or said that, you wouldn't be facing the current sad state of affairs.

But even if someone else's poor or uncalled-for behavior causes you upset, placing blame will neither change what happened nor prevent it from happening again. Instead, blaming others thrusts you into the victim role and a victim mentality; your happiness is now at the mercy of other people or happenstance. When you disable your power by blaming others, your well-being is subject to the behavior of another person or the turn of circumstances.

Being right (that is, the blameless party) doesn't always make you happy—it just makes the other party wrong. It absolves you of any complicity in the matter at hand, and it allows the unhealthy pattern to continue without you ever having to look at your own behavior.

Take your power back. Instead of reacting to someone else's behavior, be proactive. Ask yourself this question: "How have I placed myself in a position to be hurt, knowingly or not?" When you find the answer to that, you gain the knowledge you need to prevent becoming a victim again.

Perhaps you've been in the blaming habit for so long that it's difficult to see where you actually play a role in the outcome. I'll share some of my own experiences to help you view things more clearly. Once you get the hang of it, you'll find that losing this bad habit is a supereasy and liberating way to reclaim your personal power and move on.

·{ M Y S T O R Y }·

It was so easy to blame my ex-spouse for his behavior in our marriage and for being so vindictive during our divorce. I can give you countless examples to corroborate my story— and I used to be more than willing to tell anyone who would listen just how mean he was and how many ways he wronged the children and me. What I didn't know at the time was just how damaging my own behavior was when I laid all the guilt at his feet. Yes, it placed the blame on him and let others think he was a jerk, and it took the blame off poor, pitiful me. But it also kept me stuck in the victim role, which I played extremely well. It got people on my side and gave me plenty to complain about. I spent all my energy justifying why he was wrong and I was right, and it worked—people felt sorry for me. Eventually, though, it dawned on me that I volunteered to play the role of the weak, pathetic woman at the mercy of her husband's behavior. I had put myself in a seemingly helpless position by letting his actions determine my happiness. I put my own well-being in his hands, and all the while, I remained mired in a dynamic I didn't want to be in. This arrangement persisted for a long time.

To turn the situation around, I finally asked that key question, "How have I placed myself in a position to be hurt, knowingly or not, by the decisions I've made?" Notice that I didn't ask myself what he did to hurt me, nor did I complain about his actions. I asked myself to identify *my* role in the whole business. There were many ways, large and small, in which I aggravated things, such as taking his calls, getting drawn into arguments, or trying to prove he was always in the wrong. The root cause and obvious answer underlying it all was that I chose to marry him in the first place. That was on me. Of course, when I agreed to marry him, I didn't expect anything harmful to lie in our future, but the bottom line is that I made the decision to become his wife. Once I accepted that I did, in fact, have a role in our situation, my personal power returned. With personal power come options—and no situation seems hopeless when you feel you have options.

When you have a loved one dealing with addiction, you're liable to fall into the blame trap. Here are two scenarios showing how blaming your addicted loved one for your unhappiness places you in a position to be hurt.

Loaning Money. You loan them money, and they don't pay you back, which angers you. You placed yourself in the position to be harmed by loaning them the money. Yes, they are wrong not to pay you back, but the ultimate responsibility is yours. You are the one who chose to loan it to them. *Break the pattern and take your power back.* Look at your options, then behave differently the next time: for example, you can choose not to loan the money, or you can give them the loan but not get upset when they don't repay it.

The Waiting Game. You eagerly wait for them to show up at a scheduled time for a special event or meeting, (even though they rarely do), and you're crushed when they fail to appear. You placed yourself in the position to be harmed by expecting behavior from them that they haven't been capable of in the past. *Again, break the pattern and take your power back.* Don't expect them to show up. Have backup plans in place instead of waiting for them to arrive. Realize that their absence isn't a reflection on you or your worth; it's the disease talking.

Reacting Differently

It is amazingly empowering to move from a defeated or diminished position to one of strength and possibility by reversing your role from that of a victim to that of a person who can make different choices. Learning to place boundaries that protect you from being harmed works wonders to avoid disappointment and regret. (See the fuller discussion on protective boundaries in chapter 8.) You have more power than you think. *You don't need other people to behave a certain way in order for you to be okay.*

No matter how another person behaves (or how a situation turns out), your overall happiness doesn't need to be lessened. You may be disappointed, sad, or angry about what is happening, but you don't have to be paralyzed or overwhelmed. You can continue moving forward with your life.

Sometimes, the best form of reaction is no reaction. When you feel angry or frustrated with someone (in addition to blaming them), it is easy to react too quickly or to overreact, only to regret it afterward. You may wish you hadn't said or done something in haste. Perhaps you hadn't seen the situation clearly at the time, or maybe you took it way too personally. First of all, understand that everyone does this, particularly those of us who are dealing with a loved one's addiction. When you react this way, don't deride yourself; remember your worth. This particular skill takes time and patience to develop. Grant yourself some grace for not being perfect, then try to do it differently the next time. Awareness of the behavior is a kind of knowledge.

It may be wise to do (or say) nothing, at least until you're in a better place to deal with the situation and have had time to reflect on your options. Simply pausing before reacting gives you space and reduces the odds that you'll say or do something regrettable. In some circumstances, it's possible you may *never* need to do anything in response, so that can actually be the best choice. An example might be when your addict is making poor choices. Though that may be obvious, they need to figure it out for themselves. Trying to direct their life doesn't work. You think it's helpful, but it's not. They figure things out far more quickly and may even course-correct sooner without the added commentary from you.

If you choose to chime in on a situation such as this, here's a phrase I like: "I trust that you'll make the right decision." This takes you out of the equation and gives them the dignity to direct their own life.

You will feel so much more peaceful when you begin utilizing your newfound skill of not reacting immediately. It saves you in terms of angst, wasted energy, judgment, and apologies. It keeps you in a neutral position, so your relationship is likely to remain intact. You'd be surprised at how often a crisis works itself out without your assistance!

Letting Go of Resentments

Resentments can *kill* your spirit. I define resentment as any message that keeps resending itself to you. It can be something that someone said or did to you a long time ago—something that caused anger or hurt that still flickers in your mind.

Resentments are powerful and can be directed toward people, places, and things. They allow your tendency to blame others to flourish, keeping you stuck in self-righteousness, stuck in the memory of your pain and bitterness, and therefore stuck in the patterns of your life.

People will let you down. Period. It doesn't matter how much they love you, and it doesn't matter if they have the best of intentions behind their actions or words. We humans simply can't help it—we fail each other and ourselves. If you're unable to let go of the hurt, or see it from another perspective, you remain wedged between your misery and the story you create to sustain or validate it.

At some point, it will be beneficial to look at the resentments you still cling to and see how they currently impact your life. Many times, you'll find they arose during a pivotal phase of your life that fostered specific tendencies. For instance, if an alcoholic parent mistreated you in childhood and called you useless or stupid, you may be living your life according to the self-concept that formed in that early period; now, you may harbor anger toward your loved one and live with harmful tendencies such as perfectionism and people-pleasing.

It is best to review these resentments with an unbiased person or trusted adviser (such as an Al-Anon sponsor, a counselor, a coach, a spiritual adviser, or a mentor). This discussion can help you explore deeply personal matters more fully. You can work through each of your resentments, trying to see things from the other person's perspective as well as your own and watching for shortcomings in your behavior in each circumstance you review. Behavioral patterns will emerge, showing you how you have reacted in the past in ways that are counterproductive to your well-being. Armed with this information, you can devise new options that will allow you to act differently in the future. Eventually, you will loosen the chains of resentment that have restricted you for too long.

People will let you down. Period.

Working on your resentments is one of the best things you can do to take back your power and acquire serenity. It will show you where and why you developed ineffective behaviors, how they hold you back, and how you can shift your relationship to them so they no longer imprison you. You may find that it wasn't necessarily the actions of others that made you unhappy in the past but rather the way you responded to those actions.

To better understand each resentment and discover its underlying cause, explore the questions I've listed here (based in part on the work I did with a sponsor):

- **Who do you resent and why?** I resent _____ because _____. (E.g., I resent my son because he stole from me to buy drugs; I resent my mother because she chose men over me; I resent my sister because she refuses to talk to me.)
- **What fears or feelings did the resentment evoke in you?**
- **Who else did it affect?**
- **Have you spent money trying to fix it or make it better?**
- **Did it result in gender stereotyping or intimacy issues?**
- **Since the outcome of the resentment wasn't what you wanted, what outcome would you have preferred?**
- **Why might the other person have behaved so poorly?** You may feel somewhat resistant to answering this question, for you might not like or fully understand their motives. But if you're open-minded, you just might gain a little insight into *why* they've been behaving in a specific fashion. *You don't have to condone the behavior, and you don't need to justify it.* But in considering this question, you may begin to understand the hurt and fear that underlie and direct the behavior.

The offending person's behavior often says more about where they're coming from than whether they intended to harm you. Is it possible for you to acknowledge, even in a small way, that they may have been extremely stressed or acting out of fear or that they've been harmed just as much as you—and maybe even more? Some people's poor behavior is extremely selfish or bullylike because of a deep-seated fear of not having enough or being enough, or it can be due to personality changes caused by alcoholism, addiction, or mental illness. In any case, you want to observe their behavior but not judge them. This approach helps you avoid self-righteousness, making yourself right and them wrong. *You might even develop a little empathy for them.*

One tool I use when I'm really upset with someone's behavior is to pray for him or her. This can be extremely hard to do and seem contrary, but it is actually quite helpful. This is why. Instead of getting and staying really angry, if you pray for someone you can turn the table, removing yourself from a victim position and assuming an empowered one. You can do this by praying to your Higher Guidance for the person's well-being, so they won't need to react from such a painful place. In this way, you do something positive with the situation, and some of your anger will dissipate in the process, replaced with action and hope.

• **What part did you play in the resentment?** You may consider this an offensive question at first. You'd rather place all the blame on the other person. Remember, though, that when you do that, it keeps you in the victim role. By looking at your past reactions when you've been hurt or angered, you begin to notice specific behavioral patterns. In turn, this will encourage you to come up with alternative ways to deal with difficult situations and people in the future. It also will help you assess and address your own shortcomings—the behaviors that hold you back and the obstacles you place on your own path.

At this point, you can ask yourself, "Does this behavior continue to serve me, or has it become an impediment to my success?" and "How can I let go of this and behave differently?" Here are some of the biggest culprits—that is, the behaviors that contribute to your own despair: selfishness, fearfulness, self-indulgence and unrealistic expectations.

Selfishness. You want things your way. Period. Whenever you want or expect an outcome to be a certain way, *your way,* you are behaving selfishly. It doesn't mean that you don't have good reasons or that yours isn't a great idea. When two parties disagree, they're both being selfish—they both want it their way. This doesn't make one party right and the other one wrong. The lesson here is that you don't always need things to turn out your way.

Your way may not always be the best; it's just the only way you know. Beyond that, your reasoning skills are often based in fear, and they are necessarily limited. Trusting in your Higher Guidance instead of your limited perspective opens up a vast expanse of alternative, often better solutions. It allows for more options to unfold. And as mentioned earlier, having options is always a good thing.

In my experience, by letting go of an outcome you think you need, the resulting outcome is often better than you could have imagined. *If I imagine an outcome, it probably won't happen, because what usually happens is something that I never could have imagined.* You don't always need the outcome you think you do. Things can and do work out differently, and you'll be okay.

Fearfulness. You react from a place of worry or dread and make choices based on fear instead of faith. Remember, fear often arises because you're concerned that you'll lose something you already have or that you won't get something you think you need. Ask yourself, "What am I afraid of losing?" (Is it, for example, security, certainty, safety, prestige, relationships, or material items?) "What am I afraid I might not get?" (Is this a specific outcome or behavior, the perfect family, the right job, a happy ending?) What exactly are you frightened of, and how are you limiting yourself as a result? What behavior patterns have you adopted to try to alleviate fear? Do you find yourself engaging in the same behaviors (not speaking up, avoiding things, overreacting, being pessimistic, enabling, and so on) over and over again? Always keep in mind that fear can be the problem, but it cannot be the solution. Trusting your Higher Guidance is the answer when you fear things beyond your control. The antidote for fear is faith.

Self-Indulgence. Perhaps you've been concerned (and consumed) with your own interests. Have you manipulated or retaliated as a means to gain what you want at the expense of others? Have you sought coping mechanisms outside yourself to make you happy and avoid the impact of your pain, such as risky sexual encounters or an unwise use of drugs, alcohol, or money? Have you ever engaged in behaviors such as people pleasing—an act disguised as kindness—to feel better about yourself? Are you making others responsible for your emotional, physical, or spiritual health?

Unrealistic Expectations. You may be kidding yourself in believing that someone's behavior or a certain outcome could be different. Can you expect a person to suddenly change and act like you want them to? Have you denied the truth or reality of any situation? Are you really surprised when your alcoholic is drunk again? (You know what they say about doing the same thing over and over again and expecting a different outcome.)

Many behaviors are adopted—and character shortcomings created—when we attempt to protect ourselves. At some point in life, we've all been afraid but found ourselves without the tools or strategies to cope with the situation we feared; that forced us to improvise. For instance, if you had an abusive upbringing, you likely learned to keep your mouth shut to avoid being hit or yelled at. You realized that by "playing small" (being quiet and hiding away), you could protect yourself during that stage of your life. But playing small no longer serves you as an adult. Thus, the behavior that at one time might've been the only tool you had now gets in the way of your progress. And you continue to be harmed; another person harmed you years ago, but now you harm yourself by disbelieving in your true worth and letting someone else or something in the past define it. Once you are aware of this, you can reclaim your power.

The development of a behavioral imperfection doesn't mean there is something wrong with you. It simply means that you have veered off center—center being a normal behavior. From a normal, balanced position, you've either swung to the left and developed a deficiency in a specific behavior or to the right and developed an excess of that particular behavior. If, for example, you have a fear surrounding money, you may begin hoarding every penny you find (fear of losing something you already have), or you may go to the other extreme and spend frivolously and extravagantly (fear of not getting something you think you need). Another example involves courage: if this virtue is out of balance, a deficiency might result in cowardice, whereas an overabundance might result in recklessness.

When you begin to see where you tend to veer off center, you can acknowledge and recognize the reactions and behaviors that keep you stuck. You can then proceed to create alternative behaviors and reactions that will serve you better.

By the way, the following are *not* shortcomings: your weight, height, race, gender, income level, job or profession, or how your kids turn out.

To recap, here are some tips to help you avoid resentments, retain your personal power, and maintain your serenity:

- **You don't always have to be right!** Remember that when you're angry, you're probably being self-righteous. You're certain that you are right and the person who hurt you is wrong. Justifying your position drains your energy and time and leaves you unable to move forward. You don't need to be right all the time. You can be happy instead.
- **Another's behavior and actions usually have *nothing* to do with you.** Most often, they are reacting because of their own anger, past hurts, selfish motives, and so on. Repeat this statement: "It's not about me," then repeat it again and again.
- **Determine if you have placed yourself in a position to be hurt, and remove yourself from harm if possible.** Learn what you can do differently the next time to avoid being in that position again.
- **Shut the storybook.** Stop telling your story to anyone other than trustworthy counsel. When you talk to too many people, you relive your justification for being hurt over and over; you remain caught up in negativity.
- **Do you need to apologize for your behavior or forgive yourself or another?** You're not responsible for another's behavior, but you are responsible for your own.

Can you forgive? Sometimes it doesn't feel possible. When I'm dealing with this question, I remind myself of a definition I've heard: forgiveness means no longer wishing the past could have been different.

When something painful or troubling has happened, accept that fact and let go of any illusions that things might have been different. At that point, you will be able to finally move forward. Ask your Higher Guidance to help you forgive those who've wronged you. Then forgive yourself for acting in a way, or continuing to act in a way, that runs contrary to your well-being and worth. At last, you stop harming yourself.

3. STOP STEALING ALL THE GLORY

When you feel the need to take from the world, it's because you're afraid—afraid that you don't have enough and/or that you need something more or different in order to have value. You haven't truly comprehended your worth, so you compare yourself with another's talents, belongings, or life circumstance. You take what you think will fill the void, but it doesn't quite work. Nothing can fill the void except the realization of your own essence—your worth. That's what is missing. Here are some of the ways we steal from ourselves and others:

- When you put your serenity or personal power in someone else's hands, you steal from yourself.
- When you are late, you steal another's time.
- By gossiping, you steal another's reputation.
- You take away another's dignity when you feel the need to manage their lives.
- You take away your own dignity when you begin negative self-talk.
- By taking credit or denying another's recognition for a successful undertaking, you rob them of their due acknowledgment and reward.
- You steal from the world when you don't share your gifts of wisdom, time, and talents; sharing those gifts is also known as living your purpose. (*I love this one!* It helped me finish this book.) You came into this world with specific gifts. Are you using them? Even if your loved one is dealing with addiction, your gifts are still with you. Sharing them (at your job, in your hobbies, with a stranger, or in some other way) will keep you from getting caught up and totally codependent with your addict and their addiction. It will remind you that you do have something to offer that is valuable and good. When you offer it in purpose to the world, it fills you with great joy.

*When we stop asking "what's in it for me?"
and start shifting to the realization that we have
something to offer, we don't need to hide or take
from the world anymore. The question we ask
ourselves then becomes "what can I give?"*

The 3 Rs for the Soul: The Second R—Reclaiming Your Personal Power

?

.. What are you doing with what you have? Are you fully utilizing and making the most of your own talents, regardless of what's going on with another, or are you acting from a place of insufficiency by taking or withholding?

4. DISCONNECT THE DRAINERS

Are you putting your energy to good use? Where are you spending your time? What are you spending it on? If you look closely, you will see where your priorities lie. When you feel unhappy and unfulfilled, chances are you're spending time on the wrong things.

Is your life so busy that there isn't enough extra time to pursue fulfilling or fun stuff? I suspect you could benefit by simply shifting certain daily routines. By rearranging or eliminating some of them, you can make your life far more manageable, joyful, and productive. In addition to discarding the time- and energy-wasting behaviors we've already covered, including negative self-talk, stealing from others, and trying to control the uncontrollable, there are many other ways to free up some extra time. Here are things I have done myself; I find they free up not only time and energy but also money:

Limit TV. I canceled my cable television package and now watch much less TV. I got tired of dealing with cable companies, their different schemes and promotions, and the high monthly cost. It was hard at first. Yet the longer I've been without it, the more I'm glad I ditched it. I have so much more time—and money. I'm able to enjoy other things, such as reading or projects that I thought I never had time for. My head isn't crammed full of unnecessary, continually repeated information and background noise. I'm left with more time for myself, and I'm spending less time listening to society selling me the latest gadgets and pharmaceutical drugs to make me a happy person. Things have grown quite peaceful around my house.

Limit shopping. I feel heaviness when I spend money wastefully, which happens when I shop for clothes and shoes. I'm a great shopper, meaning I usually get a good deal, but sometimes, that isn't such a good thing. The temporary high that comes with the "win" of getting a great deal outweighs my need for the item at hand, and I end up with way too much stuff. There are many better places for my money that benefit me far more: my savings account, my favorite charities, even creating and promoting this book. Shopping is a never-ending, time-consuming hobby. I've grown to dislike it more and more, for the temporary high is often followed by a resounding "I really didn't need that" feeling of disappointment. *Yet there will always be another cute shirt or pair of shoes to buy. Always.*

Limit social media. Overindulging in social media is one of the biggest drains on our time and well-being. It's like putting yourself in the middle of a soap opera—full of drama and dysfunction but without any real connection or strong relationships with anyone in the real world. Many people are interested in pushing their own agenda via social media or promoting a particular image. When I cut back on both reading and posting online, I felt a lot better.

Limit certain people or relationships. Typically, a couple of people come to mind here—the ones who sap your energy, those you don't feel totally comfortable around, and those who make you want to sip tequila before they arrive. It can be hard to know how to handle this issue. It's easier to limit time with some people than with others. Unfortunately, the person you may really need to limit might be the loved one who is struggling with addiction. You don't wish to hurt their feelings or make them feel worse than they already do, of course, but time apart can help you. Their crazy behavior makes you crazy too. Your options include limiting contact for a while, keeping any interactions to a certain amount of time, and having a way to escape in mind if things start getting out of hand. Limit contact with anyone who causes you to question your worth as a result of being around them. You'll feel a great sense of relief. Take care of yourself by creating a supportive environment; surround yourself with people who value you and remind you of your goodness.

Your ability to say "no" plays a big part in taking back your personal power.

Limit your commitments. How often do you find yourself stuck in a commitment you regret? Perhaps you volunteer for a nonprofit through your employer or raise money for your child's school. Maybe you're participating in a baby shower or birthday party for an acquaintance at work. Or maybe you always host the family holiday feast. If the activity is draining you instead of exciting you, you don't have to do it: you really can say "no" sometimes! You'll find that gets easier every time you say it—no one yells at you, punishes you, or shuns you, and the world doesn't fall apart. You'll feel relieved instead of resentful. If you don't stand up for yourself and what you need, who will? Your ability to say "no" plays a big part in taking back your personal power. You get to choose what you do with your time, and when you're completely worn out, you can even opt to do nothing at all for a while. Taking care of yourself is your biggest priority. You don't have to do it all.

Medicate less. Cut back on or eliminate the mood-altering substances you consume. Can you resist the societal message that drinking alcohol is the only way to have fun? Can you ignore the pressure to consume great amounts of caffeine even though there's a coffee shop on every block? If you want to get in touch with your true self, that will be hard to do if you're always covering up who you are or numbing yourself with substances. Give some thought to the difference between spending time on activities that provide relaxation and joy versus those that obscure or alter the mind and body.

Meditate instead of worrying. Meditating will boost your spiritual knowledge of yourself more than anything I know. Instead of bombarding your mind with extraneous information or altering it with substances, hone the art of discernment. Attend to information that comes from within, from your Higher Guidance, about your circumstances and your life more generally. You don't need to take a special class or be an expert to meditate, nor is there a time limit on the practice. (See chapter 9 for a simple meditation practice.) You can easily incorporate meditation into your daily life when you cut out or reduce TV watching, shopping, social media, and alcohol and drug consumption. My first experience with meditation came with a personal challenge to commit five minutes a day to it for thirty days. I'd roll out of bed and onto my bottom first thing each morning to develop the habit.

Get outside as often as possible. Walking, working in the garden, or simply sitting and observing nature will quiet the mind and recharge your energy. It reminds you that you are part of something much bigger than yourself; there's a lot of good stuff going on around you other than what's going on in your head (flowers blooming, water running, birds singing, and dogs playing). I've learned that when my mind is racing, taking a walk outside in nature usually slows it down. In fact, this is one of my favorite therapies. What rejuvenates your energy instead of sapping it?

Cut out one bad thing from your diet, or add one good thing in. For instance, eliminate soda or sugar. Or stop eating out all the time. Add in a morning smoothie. Substitute green tea for coffee. Cut out meat for a day. Experiment. What makes you feel good? Try not to get caught up in labels—vegan, vegetarian, gluten-free, and so on. Here, as with religion, you don't have to fit into one narrow box. Learn what you like and what makes you feel your best. It doesn't matter what the latest craze or celebrity diet is. Once you get in touch with your spirituality and slow down the chatter in your head, mindful eating comes more naturally. Food will become fuel to help you live more purposefully rather than a quick fix to distract you from it.

5. LETTING GO OF PERFECT OUTCOMES

You may have heard the expressions "Just let it go" or "Let go and let God." That sounds good, but what exactly are you letting go of? Here are several possibilities:

• Letting go of any expectations for a specific outcome. Keep in mind that *expectations result in future resentments.*
• Letting go of any illusion of control you think you have.
• Letting go of any fears you have surrounding a bad outcome.
• Letting go of the misconception that you can and need to make everything turn out okay.
• Letting go of the need to have all the facts or get all of your questions answered.

Let go of the need to know. Sometimes, you just don't have to have all the answers. By thinking that you do, you drive yourself crazy trying to project various outcomes and especially worst-case scenarios, which rarely materialize. But letting go in this way is difficult to do. You want answers. For instance, if you love an addict, you want to know if they're drinking or using, where they are, if they're lying, if they showed up for work, who they're talking to on their phone, if they're passed out somewhere, if they're dying because someone beat them up, or if they're dead because of an overdose. The uncertainty drives you absolutely insane—and yet, you rarely have control over any of these things.

Let go of the need to know.

The need to know involves another illusion, another form of control. You think if you find out all the facts and get every *i* dotted and every *t* crossed, you'll be able to make the perfect decision or come up with the perfect fix; thereafter, you'll enjoy a life of unlimited happiness with only minimal pain. The trouble is, that just isn't the way it goes. Certainly, there are times when you need answers in order to take the next step, but resorting to behaviors such as spying on your loved one's phone or email, measuring the alcohol, calling others to get information, and searching for clues is unproductive. Your energy is better spent making those changes that you can for yourself instead.

This tenet applies to other areas in your life as well, including your spirituality. If you wait to have all the answers or if you keep looking for something concrete such as a specific sign, you might never find a Higher Guidance to hold on to. You'll never have answers for everything, at least not in this lifetime. Rather, you'll figure things out by learning as you go along. The need to know every little detail before acting will keep you stuck where you are instead of accepting some uncertainty and flowing into your own life. You learn that you can still go forward with your day instead of being emotionally held hostage by outside influences or another's actions.

When you accept and even welcome uncertainty, you are free to take risks, without the fear of making mistakes. You won't feel constrained by a need to adhere to one or two specific plans of action. You can experiment, investigate, change course, imagine, create, and more. Letting go liberates you to live your life as only you can. Instead of trying to play it safe in everything you do and orchestrating your life in a seemingly failsafe manner, you are freed to experience the exquisiteness of life as it unfolds.

The truth is that everything is constantly changing and you have very little control over most of it. When you learn to let go of those things you can't control, on one hand, and control the things you can, on the other (becoming your best self), life gets a whole lot easier. You will still forget, from time to time, that things work better this way and try to grab control again. But then you'll become miserable once more—and let it go again. This vicious cycle will persist until you fully trust that no matter what happens, you will be okay.

·{ MY STORY }·

One day while walking, I was upset that I didn't seem to have any direction for my future. I asked the God of my understanding, "What do you *want* from me?"—meaning "What is it you want me to do with my life?" I don't always receive insights, but on that day, I did, which is why I still remember it so clearly: *Cyndee, you don't need to know the future and here's why ...*

1. You simply wouldn't believe or understand it (right now).

2. You aren't prepared for it yet.

3. You wouldn't live in the present if you always knew the future.

Think about this last one. If you *did* know what the future held, your response would be to begin projecting forward, asking even more "what ifs." Not only would you not be living in the present, you'd also be projecting, imagining, planning, and scheming for a future beyond the future that isn't even here yet!

Ask yourself this question: "Would knowing the answer (to anything) fundamentally change who I am as a worthy, divine child of the Universe?" If you knew your loved one was drinking or cheating, what aspect of your divinity would that change? You might indeed need to make some changes in the future in regard to your living arrangements, money matters, and so forth, but that wouldn't change your fundamental value as a human being. Can you see the difference? Would it change any of your innate talents or passions—or extinguish the light inside you? It shouldn't, unless you depend on another's behavior to determine who you are instead of exploring for yourself with the help and trust of Higher Guidance.

I used to think, *If I just had a time frame, if I only knew a date that I could survive up to and after that things would get better, life would be a lot easier.* But that kind of thinking suggests that the whole time up to the point of change I'd be hanging on by my fingernails, right? Things don't need to work that way. You *don't* have to be miserable until things change; otherwise, you'd miss out on a lot of life. When you find yourself enduring the present, waiting for things to get better, instead of participating in life, ask yourself this question: "What is it that I'm not accepting right now because I want it to be different?" The answer is usually the exact thing that you need to stop trying to change or make different.

≡ The universe is made up of experiences that are designed to burn out your attachment, your clinging, to pleasure, to pain, to fear, to all of it. And as long as there is a place where you're vulnerable, the universe will find a way to confront you with it.

—Unknown

Isn't this a great saying? It reminds me that I need to address the things that keep blocking me in the pursuit of myself; if I don't, they'll always be a thorn in my side. Whenever I have dared to let go of an outcome I wanted (or the only outcome I could imagine that I thought was good), again and again things turned out differently—*better than my mind could've perceived.* The more I can let go and trust that it will work out, accepting that I don't need to know how, the more grounded and sane I am amid uncertainty.

•.. Haven't we all been faced with a character trait or behavior that always seems to pop up and cause us to stumble? Can you think of yours?

Take a look at what you're attached to and recognize these attachments as obstacles that keep you from moving forward. You can be attached to any of the following (and more):

• Expectations about how things should be or how they should turn out (attributes of a perfect spouse, a loved one's life turning out a specific way)
• Your substitute self, including your past stories and beliefs
• Resentments
• Coping mechanisms

·{ MY STORY }·

After my divorce, I clung to my role as a stay-at-home mom. That's all I had known for the previous fourteen years, and I loved it. I didn't know who I was without that part to play. It took me quite a while to realize I could love and give to my children but also share my time and talents with others. Until then, though, I really mourned the loss of that role, that period in my life, and the relationship I had with my kids. For a long time afterward, the only thing I wanted was to be that mom again, the one they adored before all the divorce chaos ensued and while they were still under my influence. But I wasn't in that role anymore, and I couldn't imagine ever again finding anything as good as I'd enjoyed. At the time, I didn't know that I was more than that role. And I didn't realize that I could be a good mom even if I wasn't the stay-at-home kind.

As I gradually became open to change instead of fighting it, I learned that letting other aspects of my personality flourish was okay too. I came to understand that the fighting is what makes you miserable—*the pain you feel comes from your resistance to accepting what is.* I now realize that the clinging to my former role came from my fear of the unknown. Since that time, I have been through enough change to know that a current tumultuous situation is not a predictor of future happiness, or lack thereof. Change allows us to explore other aspects of ourselves, that's all. We can fight it or we can accept it, but we can't avoid it.

The Freedom of Personal Choice

As you focus your trust in a Higher Guidance and begin to control those things that you can, you'll continue to discover aspects of yourself that you never knew existed. Your work in rethinking your religion and reclaiming your power also opens the door to many other areas in your life that you can revisit and revise, based on your new relationship with personal truth and trust.

How many of the following things might change as a result of your greater self-knowledge?

• Past ideas of success and power
• The illusion of the perfect family, perfect body, perfect life
• Assumed responsibilities
• Your views on aging and the premium placed on youth
• Political affiliations
• Current friendships
• Relationships with family members
• How you exercise—is going hard and fast always the answer?
• Your job—is it time to change?
• How you spend your time—your hobbies, commitments, and relaxation time
• Your reactions—are they productive or destructive?
• Any discriminatory or prejudicial beliefs or practices
• How you dress—are you dressing for a role?
• Your daily consumption of stuff (information, purchases, TV, and so forth)
• What you put into your body—are you overmedicating or eating poorly?
• Societal expectations—how you feel about the way you've always done things

When it comes to deciding what changes to make for yourself, sometimes it's helpful to look at the motivation behind your behavior. Are you doing something because ...

1. You're succumbing to outside pressure?
2. It makes you feel superior?
3. You want others to perceive you in a certain way?
4. It's just the way you've always done it (holiday traditions, cable TV, and so on)?
5. You just really enjoy it?

The first three motivations are based on manipulation; the fourth might be based on a worn-out pattern that is now unnecessary. The first four are areas ripe for change. The fifth one indicates that you don't need to change a thing unless the behavior is causing harm.

Here are some of the changes that happened in my life as a result of rethinking my religion and reclaiming my power—the first two of the 3 Rs. A lot of these examples may seem simple or even frivolous, but they mattered to me in terms of time, expense, and especially the ability to choose for myself. *Being able to place your personal brand on your life is precious.* You don't always need to do things the way your parent did or the way society-at-large suggests you should. Your freedom to make such changes gives others permission to do the same.

• **I took off my fake fingernails.** I didn't need them in order to feel happy or successful. I was foolish to believe I enhanced my worth by wearing them.

• **I stopped having my toenails painted.** This was a big deal because as a yoga teacher, my feet were always on display. But I wanted to show my students that we don't have to follow societal expectations. Painted toes or fingers have nothing to do with using our talents, enjoying others, and living life. I still love painted toes: I think they're pretty and expressive. Yet I continue to leave mine plain, as a personal reminder to myself that I'm okay just as I am.

• **I stopped perming and curling my hair.** I let it be as straight as it naturally is. I don't have it dyed, and I keep it long so I don't have to be a slave to getting it done so often.

• **I cut monthly expenses.** I canceled my cable TV, decreased the cost of my cell phone plan, and got rid of my home phone service. This saved me about $250 a month. I'm so glad I did this! Without the cable, I watch much less TV, which means I have time for many other things.

• **I didn't let my college degree restrict my job choices.** I'm not employed in an occupation that matches my college degree (accounting). No doubt, I could make more money if I were, so I struggled with this decision until I finally realized that I'm not utilizing my greatest gifts by sitting behind a desk and working with numbers. I'm a visionary, a big-picture person. Once I figured this out, I understood why I felt I was diagonally parked in a parallel universe when I worked in the corporate world. I'm good with details, but I'd prefer not to dwell in them.

- **I have fun with my clothing.** My clothes are colorful, the bolder the better. Wearing them just makes me happy. Living in Colorado, I love being outdoors and being active. I don't dress up very much, but I get a kick out of it when I do. I don't need to wear the latest fashion to fit in. In fact, if everyone else is purchasing the "in" fashion, that's the best reason for me to run the other way. I don't want to be like everyone else. The way we dress is such a huge area for self-expression.

- **I don't overdo it when drinking alcohol.** We feel a subtle pressure to drink when we're at a party or out with others, but if I don't feel like drinking, I don't. When I do partake, it's often minimal because that's what works for me.

- **I set boundaries with my cell phone.** I often mute my phone so I'm not disturbed. I do this when I'm meditating, when I need to be productive, and when I'm sleeping. If I'm in the middle of something during the day, I let calls go to voice mail until I have time to deal with them. I used to think that I needed to be available to everyone, night and day. I don't anymore. I'm not that important, plus I realized that if I'm not always available, others in my life may work on their problems themselves instead of relying on me to solve them. If it's important, they'll leave a message.

- **I'm stingy with my time.** If I'm invited to an event I'd rather not attend, I say no. I don't rationalize why I should go and then get resentful later, and I don't feel guilty that I didn't go. I value my time. I don't need to spend it doing things I don't enjoy or hanging out with people I don't care for unless it's absolutely necessary.

- **I cut back on shaving.** I never shave the tops of my legs anymore. I rather like them the way they are (it helps that I'm not a hairy person). When my sister-in-law started doing this, I thought it was a great idea, so I decided to join her. It was a good decision.

- **I minimize the makeup.** I very rarely wear makeup anymore. I credit my yoga teachers and a few friends for setting the example and giving me the courage to go without it.

- **I speak my piece.** I'm getting better at understanding how I feel, and I find I can articulate what's on my mind without wanting to justify or alter my position for the benefit of others. I don't need to impose my ideas on them or have them think the way I do. I am also learning that I don't always have to speak up when it won't serve any purpose (though I still need some work in this area).

- **I embrace spirituality.** I'm always open to new teachings, and I love delving deeper into something that resonates with me. I stopped attending the last formal church I belonged to, but I've found other ways that help me feel spiritually uplifted and guided. I read spiritual stuff like crazy. I usually find a nugget or two that I can add to my own understanding.

- **I reassessed my political affiliation.** I changed my lifelong political association to "Unaffiliated." I like the freedom to vote as I wish and the independence that comes from not feeling I need to vote along any party line.

- **I cut back on Christmas decorations.** At Christmastime, I put up a tree with lights and garland only. I stopped using ornaments once my kids were older and didn't care about them—or didn't care to help put them up or take them down. No one is suffering, and it cuts down on holiday stress to boot.

- **I cut out the holiday ham.** I hate ham and the gross white gravy that comes from it. No more for us. Now we experiment with nontraditional holiday dishes like lobster butter over pasta, crab legs, and homemade lasagna. We make whatever sounds good and is different from our ordinary fare.

All these things work for me. They've simplified my life, provided expression for my personality, and saved me time and money. None of them are necessarily right or wrong, but prior to making these changes, my efforts tilted toward meeting the expectations of others and tailoring my actions in order to be accepted. I spent way too much time on things that didn't matter, instead of actually doing what mattered to me.

? .. Where else might you be living with worn-out beliefs or practices that no longer serve your well-being?

7

The 3 Rs for the Soul: The Third R—Releasing Your Personal Essence

Living Your Life—As Only You Can

Every single person has a gift to give the world—including you. Contrary to what you might feel as a result of being enmeshed in a loved one's addiction, *your presence in the world matters*. External achievements, circumstances, or perceived failures have nothing to do with the human connection you can offer to another human being. The world needs your love and your talents—even though your addict may reject them.

Two universal questions are often asked: "How do I find meaning in my life?" and "What is my purpose?" Many self-help books and motivational seminars address these very topics. This book is one such resource. *Finding purpose in your life is very different from finding your life's purpose.* There are many ways to achieve the first goal; there is only one way to achieve the second. Finding meaning comes from purposeful living—knowing your worth and then making your life decisions based on a deep trust in yourself and your Higher Guidance (the first and second of the 3 Rs). As a result, you feel liberated and comfortable in sharing your light with others you meet in your various life experiences. There is no dissonance or misalignment between your natural state and your actions. A mistake many people make is searching high and low for their one and only life purpose, assuming that when they find it, they'll also have found their worth.

Worth comes first. Don't put the cart before the horse. Work on your self-worth before seeking your purpose. If you truly come to believe you add value because of your existence on the planet, purpose and meaning will come far more easily.

Gurus, Self-Help Books, and Seminars Don't Always Work

Have you ever been "wowed" by a motivational reading or speaker and resolved to change your life from that point forward? Have you then been disappointed when your enthusiasm dissipates slowly over the next week or two? Why does that happen?

As excited as you might be about finding an answer, your staying power can be compromised. Two underlying factors may prevent you from creating change in your life:

1. **You're not in enough pain to change.** There is strange comfort in discomfort, if that's what you know and are used to living with. It typically takes those who love an addict a very long time before they change. You have to be in the situation long enough to see that what you're doing now, as well as all that you've done in the past, hasn't helped. Only when you cross a certain pain threshold (which is different for everyone) will you be willing to step out of your discomfort zone and do things differently. Until then, you'll remain vigilant in your current efforts, you'll stop living your own life, and you'll forget your worth and no longer believe that you could possibly have anything meaningful to offer the world.

2. **You try to change the wrong things.** The modification you're trying to achieve doesn't address the underlying need or resonate with you at a deep level. You may convince yourself that it will be helpful, but it will only be a distraction. It's like going to the hardware store for a loaf of bread—you'll never find it there. You're going to the wrong place for what you need. As a result, any change you manage to make will be short-lived, and the main problem will persist.

When you are part of a group of likeminded individuals, all excited to better their lives, there is enormous collective energy. This force becomes infectious and continues to build as you anticipate being given the magic answer(s) that will finally allow you to overcome all the barriers and obstacles that have previously held you back. Except they don't.

Personal change doesn't come from outside oneself. At some point, you must do the work. Change is an inside job. Someone else's motivational techniques or passion can never substitute for your own internal desires and passion. Gathering information is necessary, but focusing your attention on anything other than that which resonates with you at a deep level will not bring lasting change. The temporary high you achieve by believing you found an answer for all your problems begins to wear off, and reality sets in.

Change is an inside job.

Your Greatest Gifts: They Aren't Always What You Think

This inspiration came when I read a specific Bible verse, Romans 12:6–8, which says: "We have different gifts, according to the grace given us. If a man's gift is prophesying, let him use it in proportion to his faith. If it is serving, let him serve; if it is teaching, let him teach; if it is encouraging, let him encourage; if it is contributing to the needs of others, let him give generously; if it is leadership, let him govern diligently; if it is showing mercy, let him do it cheerfully."

This passage made me rethink what gifts and talents actually are, and it helped me see that I had totally misunderstood my own. They are much broader and more universally applicable than I had previously believed. I also realized that you can use your gifts to encourage others, in whatever capacity you may find yourself!

Gifts and talents can be cultivated, but they are innate, which means they are inherent within you. They don't need to be taught, though some can be honed. I've since found that one of my particular talents is teaching. I can articulate my thoughts and explain things to others fairly well, and I enjoy doing it. I can learn and refine my knowledge of the topic I want to teach, but the gift of teaching is already there.

You may seek new direction in your life as your willingness to rethink things expands and you comprehend your worth. Difficulty and change often go hand in hand. You may find yourself wondering, "What's next?" or "What do I want to do with the rest of my life?" If you don't have a clue, that's okay. You don't have to force anything or have it all figured out.

Your situation might require a big change or several small ones. As long as you're committed to allowing change within you, whatever changes you make will guide you on your journey, culminating in more ways to use your gifts and talents in purposeful endeavors.

So what are your gifts and talents? And are you using them in your vocation, your hobby, or somewhere else in your life? Once a sense of purpose begins to weave its way into all aspects of your life and you find a way to express your specific talents and gifts into the world, you have found your purpose: that is your life purpose.

Connected by a Thread: The Dots in Your Life

Perhaps you can't imagine what your callings in life are. Often, they're not what you might've chosen or even vaguely what you've envisioned. But life has prepared you for them along the way. When you've lived long enough, you can look back at your life and find a connecting thread through many of your life events (the dots). It connects one dot to another. You may have originally thought the dots represented random events, but each event actually requires the prior event to have occurred. Look at the threads in your life and see if you can connect the dots or notice any patterns. My dots connect like this:

1. I had a part-time job at a stock brokerage that worked with my kids' school schedule (9:00 a.m. to 1:00 p.m., Monday through Friday, with summers and holidays off). That job lasted for only a short while before they did away with those specific work hours, but I did manage to get my Series 7 License (Registered Representative, enabling me to sell mutual funds and stocks) while I worked there.

2. I was getting divorced and needed to find a full-time position. My soon-to-be ex-husband got into a conversation with a stranger in an athletic club locker room and found the man was looking to hire someone with a Series 7 License. I got the job. I ended up having a couple of really fabulous mentors at the company, and they both had great confidence in me at a time when I didn't have any in myself. I'll never forget their support. In hindsight, it was a top-notch company with top-notch people who taught me how to succeed in financial sales. This job worked on straight commission. As a single mom, I worked really hard and would cold-call anybody. Failing wasn't an option.

3. I met an interesting man through a guy I was dating. I hoped he might be a prospective client.

4. The idea of publishing a magazine to support divorced people began to excite me. I knew how much my family had suffered during my divorce, and I figured other people might need help when they were going through the same thing. I quit my financial sales job and

began creating the magazine. I loved the work. It allowed me to use my imagination in so many ways, and information gleaned about the topic proved therapeutic. Of course, the only way I could have brought this magazine into existence was based on two previous dots: I had to have gone through a divorce, and I had to know how to cold-call people, as advertising sales supported the magazine.

5 I sold the magazine after three years, not knowing what was next. I married the interesting man from Dot 3.

6 I got a full-time job in product development at another financial institution near my home. It became obvious after two months that the job wasn't quite as advertised. I decided to quit, but before I left, I was hired by a senior vice president to work in a different area of the company. It turns out he was in my spin class. I had no idea we worked at the same company.

7 My new job seemed like a much better fit, but no one was around to train me there either, and no one seemed to know how to utilize my skills. I made the decision to quit if I couldn't turn things around by the one-year mark. When that day came, I handed in my notice.

8 My son's addiction had spiraled out of control. He finally agreed to seek help. My last day at work was on a Friday, and the following Monday, I took my son to his first drug rehab in Arizona. The timing worked out quite well, since I didn't have to return to a job and his addiction-caused crises had totally exhausted me.

9 I didn't know exactly what to do when I returned home, but I realized I had to take care of myself. I enrolled in a yoga teacher-training program. I didn't necessarily plan to become a teacher; I just thought yoga might help me, and I wanted to learn it correctly. I wasn't sure I had the ability to complete the program because I was such a mess emotionally and physically and so entangled in my son's addiction. My teacher empathized, and, as I related earlier, she encouraged me to stay on. Her generous offer provided the freedom I needed to get started on a new journey.

10 I reluctantly began attending Al-Anon meetings at the suggestion of my son, who had been in the AA program. I finally met some people who understood what it was like to live with an addict. I got a sponsor and went through the Twelve Steps.

11 I ended up teaching yoga. First, I volunteered at a drug and alcohol rehab center in town, with a few other odd teaching gigs on the side. Then, I took over the corporate yoga program at the financial institution I had resigned from not long before. I never would have imagined things turning out that way—and I loved it!

12 One of my favorite parts of teaching yoga was writing the lessons I would teach before the class did any actual poses. These lessons were both spiritual and practical in nature, and they were based on aspects of yoga philosophy, as well as AA's Twelve Steps. I was amazed at the changes I'd observed in myself and eager to share my tools with others. So I fashioned them into a relatable format that my students could easily apply to their circumstances and incorporate into their lives. Many yoga teachers don't include lessons as part of their classes, but I discovered that the students gobbled up the messages of hope that were offered to them. Many made major changes in their lives as a result of connecting with themselves on a much deeper level. I kept a copy of most of these lessons, thinking I might want to put them together someday. They became the genesis for this book.

13 I took five weeks off from my job teaching yoga to compile my lessons and thoughts into a book. At the end of the five weeks, I went back to teaching, although I had found I liked putting the book together. I wanted to pursue the book project but wondered how I might free up more time to devote to it.

14 A couple of months later, I found out that a corporate wellness company was going to take over all the exercise classes where I worked, including the yoga classes. I could still teach, but I'd be working under their umbrella instead of running the program myself; moreover, my hourly rate would be reduced. All this seemed to signal that it was the right time for me to leave and continue writing the book full-time.

To summarize:

- Divorce took me to a top financial company
- My financial sales experience and divorce experience led to *Divorce in Denver Magazine—Moving Forward*
- Sale of the magazine led to a product development job at another financial company
- I married the man to whom my ex-boyfriend introduced me

- My son's drug addiction led to my yoga teacher training
- His drug addiction also led me to Al-Anon and becoming an Al-Anon sponsor
- Yoga teacher training led to running the yoga program at my prior employer's offices
- All the preceding experiences led to me writing this book, utilizing my personal knowledge about divorce, loving an addict, and yoga philosophy as well as my teaching experience and Twelve Step sponsorship (I also hope my sales and marketing experience will prove helpful in getting this book's message out)
- What's next?

Your Callings in Life

Sometimes, you have more than one calling in your lifetime: it's not necessarily a "one-and-done" kind of thing. When I finally got to the point of publishing *Divorce in Denver Magazine*, I thought that was it. I'd finally found my calling, my one and only true purpose. But then I tired of it a few years later, which really frightened me. I feared I'd never have another calling, that I was doomed and relegated to whatever job I could scavenge up.

I was wrong. Life just keeps preparing you for the next thing. I had to go through many more experiences before the next calling was laid before me, and then I had to gather the courage to step into it.

Looking back, can you see the thread that connects the dots in your life? Can you see where one thing had to have taken place in order for the next thing to occur? You may even find that some of them have led you back to something you loved early on or something that you always felt a natural affinity for. Life has a way of calling you back to things that resonated with you in your younger days. Could it be that you were already in touch with your innate gifts and talents before they were swept to the side in the rush of everyday life or buried under societal expectations?

Keep your mind and options open as you move forward. The future may look far different than you ever expected or imagined. Way back when, I wouldn't have guessed in a million years that I would one day publish a magazine or write a book about healing from a loved one's addiction. The hardest issues in my life and the darkest of times have created unbelievable opportunities for growth. These issues uncovered and nurtured gifts I never knew were mine. The same will happen for you.

Playing Small Won't Keep You Safe: Experiment with Life

You cannot purchase experience or wisdom. They can only be earned as a result of living life, enduring situations that stretch your capability to handle them, and learning as you go. Everything you encounter will teach you something, no matter how big or small. If you fail to learn the lesson, it'll keep coming back in various forms to visit you until you figure it out.

Part of reclaiming your personal presence and standing strong in the personal knowledge of self involves self-study, that is, discovering what works best for you and you alone: for your body, your mind, and your spirit. For instance, consider your eating habits. You might experiment with vegetarianism or a gluten-free diet to see how your body responds, or you might create your own combination plan that works better for you. Play with the possibilities, but don't feel beholden to anything specific that society deems wonderful at the time if it doesn't work for you.

Refine what you put into your mind. Notice how differently you feel if you read a women's or men's magazine marketing a specific brand of beauty versus reading an uplifting book or doing a crossword puzzle. Try going without the news for a week and see if you notice a change.

Seek different modalities for connecting with your spiritual side—various types of meditation, a new style of yoga, finding a new church or dumping your old one, hiking, gardening, dancing, and more. Choosing a career or vocation that allows expression of your spiritual gifts will be enormously fulfilling.

Establishing boundaries with your addicted loved one (and others) is a huge area for experimentation. Learn which boundaries are critical to your well-being and determine how to best put them in place. Read more about protective boundaries in chapter 8.

Living life too cautiously for fear of making a misstep won't keep you safe; it will stifle your creativity and dim your light. You can cocoon yourself and attempt to play it safe by adhering to the latest expert's advice. You can make the most conservative decisions possible to avoid risking failure or embarrassment in any endeavor. But the challenges of life will still find you.

By testing things out, you learn what best aligns you with your own energy and wellness. You don't need to care about the latest trends or what others around you are doing. *You* choose what's best for you, and the only way to gain that wisdom is through experimentation.

The truth is, bad things are going to happen regardless (and good things as well), but playing small won't save you from them. It only keeps you confined, stunting your personal growth. And you still get old and die.

If fear of failure is the only reason you're choosing not to act, then it's not a good enough reason. So many times in life, you're afraid to go after big things, to put yourself "out there" on a limb that feels shaky. You come up with a million different ways that a bold move won't work and then convince yourself that you shouldn't even try. You're afraid, that's all. Yet by not trying, you've already failed.

For example, you may put off diving into something new because you think you aren't ready. There will be many things that you'll never be ready for, but that doesn't mean you can't do them. Just go ahead and try. It can be a little scary, but it is also strangely exhilarating to step into the unknown and trust that you'll be okay. To give you an idea of what this looks like, here are three examples from my own life:

- **Teaching yoga.** I could've attended multiple training programs to try to feel ready to teach when I was a new yoga instructor. But the fact is, I never would have felt ready *enough*. The only way I really learned how to teach was by actually teaching. Being taught how to teach (or learn any endeavor) only takes us so far. Working with students and incorporating our personality into our teaching is how we find our groove. No teacher I've ever known feels like they are fully ready. Looking back, I would've missed out on some wonderful experiences if I had played it safe and never taught that first class.
- **Coaching and mentoring.** I could have put off mentoring people in Al-Anon until I felt I had everything together (which would never happen) or waited to coach until I had a "coaching certificate" from one of the numerous companies that offer them. Those companies might have taught me their way of doing things, in addition to taking my money and time, but I would still need to *do* the coaching myself to figure out what works. Again, knowledge can help us, but it doesn't substitute for actually doing something uncomfortable and learning from the experience.

• **Writing.** Right now, I could be taking multiple writing workshops and devouring books about how to be a better writer. Believe me, I've wasted plenty of time doing just that. Though I was gaining some knowledge, it distracted me from the actual work of writing. What I needed to do was sit down and write, sharing knowledge from my perspective and voice without comparison to other books or writers. There will be people, no doubt, who don't like this book, who disagree with my ideas, who don't like me personally, and so on, but I'm writing the book anyway. I'm willing to accept any criticism that comes my way because I know this volume will help someone else. I'm not going to play small anymore simply because I'm afraid.

One template does not work for all. You accumulate wisdom with each person you meet and each experience you live through. Your insight and intuition kick in when you put yourself out there and there's nowhere to hide. You must trust that you will be okay. The Universe supports you in your endeavors if you are in close contact with your Higher Guidance. When you're heading into a scary situation, it helps to remember this: *it's not all about you.* Instead, ask yourself what you can give to the person or situation you're dealing with. You don't need to seek perfection. You just need to be willing to share your knowledge in order to help and serve others in the best way your gifts allow. Human genuineness is valued far more by others than human perfection.

Going Forward Afraid: Finding Inspiration, Passion, and the Fire in Your Belly

When you are inspired by some great purpose, some extraordinary project, all your thoughts break their bonds; your mind transcends limitations, your consciousness expands in every direction, and you find yourself in a new, great and wonderful world. Dormant forces, faculties and talents become alive, and you discover yourself to be a greater person by far than you ever dreamed yourself to be.

—Attributed to Patanjali (source unknown)

As you begin to discover what ignites the spark in your personality, the following tips might prove helpful:

- **You will never think your way to a purpose.** Purpose comes only from personal action; you must engage in something.

There is no need to ask your friends or take any more tests. In doing so, you are looking for one of two things: (1) support to reinforce or validate what you already know you should do or want to do, or (2) outside information to help you define yourself. Both serve as distractions that encourage you to avoid the real work of looking within yourself to find out what inspires you.

Notice clues along the way. What do you love to talk and read about? What do you spend your money on? (Examples here might include specialty magazine subscriptions, training sessions, retreats, or events.) What would you spend time doing if you could do anything you wished?

You must learn how to quiet your mind in order to identify and trust your deeper longings because your ego will continually tell you why you're not good at something and why you shouldn't even attempt it; this, in turn, can make you afraid to proceed to the experiential part of trying something different. You must *do* something. You must act and take a chance on something. Even if you fail, it won't be a waste of time at all, for any failure still brings knowledge.

Sometimes, you can clarify your preferences by trying a bunch of things or approaches and eliminating what you don't like—a narrowing down process, if you will. Failure is a necessary part of this process too. When something doesn't go as planned, you learn to adjust so it will work out better in the future or you discard it if it doesn't suit you. You might start down one path and end up on another, but you would never have found that second path if you hadn't tried the first.

If everything always goes smoothly, there can be no growth, no insight, and no reason to get excited. *Failure is a necessary component, and courage brings about the opportunity.*

- **Never give up on something you think about every day.** What was on your mind prior to the turmoil of addiction, your loveless marriage, or your hectic career? Is there something you used to think about that brought you excitement or joy? Do you love to cook for others, test new recipes, refinish furniture, dance like a fool, or drive fast cars? Is there a particular activity that invigorates you and causes you to lose track of time, such as coaching a youth sport or running marathons for charity and thereby creating change for people in need? Do you allow these passions a place in your life? If not, maybe it is time for you to put a greater emphasis on incorporating them into your regular activities. Perhaps you simply long for some peace, normalcy, stability, spare time, energy, or freedom? Make time for those things that bring you great joy by disconnecting the drainers, as we talked about previously. You often leave your passions behind when chaos surrounds you, but they are great and necessary reminders that good things still exist.

• **What is most personal is also universal.** The experiences you go through help you accumulate knowledge that can benefit others and lessen their pain and suffering. Remember that others have been there too. Reach out to them. There's a reason why people form support groups when bad things happen (MADD, Al-Anon, and a host of others). There is a special camaraderie that only exists among people who've endured similar situations; they can both learn from and support one another. When you can be open about your loved one's addiction, you'll be amazed at how many other people are dealing with similar circumstances and could use a friend.

Don't Be Afraid to Put Your Work (Your Gifts and Talents) into the World

As I write this book, I can attest to the feelings of fear that arise around sharing one's self and one's work with the world—the shaky voice and hands, the sweaty armpits, and the shortness of breath you experience when you begin to share your ideas with others and anxiously await their reaction. These feelings are normal, and they often accompany any new endeavor that stretches you into the unknown.

What is this paralyzing fear that causes most of us to stop in our tracks and say, "Whoa, hold on! I'd rather go back into my comfortable rut?"

Your biggest fear is that others will judge you as harshly as you have judged yourself. They'll think you're a fraud, that you don't have anything worthwhile to contribute. They'll get up and walk out; they won't pay attention; they'll decide your products or services are useless; they'll give you a bad review. No one will ever recommend you or want to hear from you again. Your friends and family members will be embarrassed and distance themselves. No one will want anything to do with you. You'll end up all alone and die with no one to love you or care about you. Have thoughts like these ever gone through your mind?

Of course, such thoughts are baseless and even ridiculous, and most of you know that by now because of the work you've done with your Higher Guidance. Any potential criticism, rejection, or disassociation has nothing to do with your worth as a human being. But at the same time, the feedback can provide information that will make you and your products and services even better. It can teach you how to refine, improve, or retool whatever you're working on.

You must put yourself into unknown situations in order to grow and learn. Hiding in your rut to avoid any perceived judgment or condemnation also keeps you from doing anything spectacular or amazing.

Why should you dare to venture out and risk public ridicule and humiliation? Because it's what you're meant to do. Everything in your life has brought you to this place—the knowledge you've gained, the talents you've honed, and the disasters and losses you've endured. Failing to step out and use your gifts and talents would minimize your presence on the planet. Not only that, it would make you selfish, for you're withholding your gifts and talents from the world. You have something to share that can benefit others. You must do it in some way, shape, or form while you still can.

No doubt, you *will* be afraid. Fear is real, and you can't avoid it entirely. Do you know that the thing people most often fear is being afraid? Facing the fear can actually be harder than confronting what's on the other side of it.

?.. What are you not doing because of fear? How are you letting fear hold you back—whether it's dealing with your loved one or making other life choices?

Plugging In: Connecting with Community and Friends

Bonding and connecting with others in a likeminded, supportive community is extremely important for your well-being.

Everyone needs a mix of time spent alone and time spent with others. The ratio depends on your personality. You may have a tendency to isolate yourself if you're dealing with addiction. Your energy is likely down, you're unsettled and uncertain, and you don't feel that you have anything uplifting to share. This may be the exact time to get out and be with friends, neighbors, and others.

The world is full of incredible people who have felt broken and have much wisdom to share. Being involved with them can provide great comfort.

Within a supportive group of acquaintances, you are more likely to be at ease in expressing who you are, even if you're not at your best; after all, they're not always at their best either. Connecting with others reminds you that you're not alone, and it lets you feel you're a part of something bigger than yourself. It can help your current ills seem less powerful and show you that goodness and laughter still exist in the world even though you've forgotten them temporarily. It can be a reminder that others often have greater problems than you; you can learn from those who've been in your shoes. The world is full of incredible people who have felt broken and have much wisdom to share. Being involved with them can provide great comfort.

Finding the right group of people is important. Some of these people will become vital in challenging and supporting you and helping you grow.

Two of the communities I'm involved in, as previously mentioned, are Al-Anon and yoga. Although I don't believe exactly the same way as others in either group, they support my growth and help me to see the world differently. One of the reasons I like both groups is because of the divergent thinking and acceptance I find in them. I feel free to express my innermost thoughts, fears, and questions without being judged.

Your communities, groups, and friends are likely to change over time. For instance, many parents coach a child's team or volunteer in the classroom when they are in the full throes of parenting and then move on as their kids get older. Some of your interests will wane and change, and some will always hold your fancy. Don't be afraid to let some of them go to make room for something new.

A Group I Never Wanted to Be Part Of—Al-Anon

I did not want to go to an Al-Anon meeting. That's what most people say. We aren't the ones with the problem; it's our loved one who has the issue. But most of us who sit in the meetings have reached our own bottom, and we don't know what else to do. We realize that our lives have become unmanageable. We are suffering greatly.

I had always thought I could find my way out of a box; I'm good at finding creative solutions. Not this time. My son's addiction took my legs out from under me. I totally lost myself trying to save him—and it didn't help.

I first read the Twelve Steps when I attended an Alcoholics Anonymous meeting that my son was leading. I was surprised at the time. The steps were so basic and understandable, not what I expected at all. My first thought was that the world would be a better place if everyone lived by those guidelines. I still believe that.

I came away with two important pieces of information from the initial meeting of Al-Anon I attended, at the urging of my son. First, my life had become unmanageable (as stated in the first step). I knew that life wasn't going the way I'd anticipated, but the word *unmanageable* fit perfectly. Second, I learned about the "Three Cs": I didn't cause it, I can't control it, and I can't cure it. Wow! That had a huge impact on me. It helped me to know that I wasn't responsible for my loved one's addiction. I could lay that burden down. Some people also add a fourth C to the mix: I can complicate it.

Addiction doesn't discriminate. In every Al-Anon group I've been in, I've found people from all walks of life; from company presidents to administrative assistants, television news anchors, and the unemployed. I love the diversity. It's a group of people who share a common bond, one that I never knew about or wanted to be a part of until I realized these people had dealt with similar circumstances; indeed, some had dealt with situations much worse than mine—and they had survived. Now they were even able to laugh. How foreign that seemed to me.

The meetings are touching and real because all the people in the room are dealing with the brutal reality of addiction. They are raw and vulnerable; they have tried everything they knew about to manage and control their lives, only to find nothing worked. There is no room for pretense in these meetings, just the damn sad truth. And that often includes legal issues, prison sentences, lost jobs, adultery, divorce, suicidal behavior, and death. These people have often spent a whole lot of money trying to save their loved ones—covering medical bills, making their addicts' overdue payments, paying for their stays at rehab centers, and on and on.

Al-Anon is a spiritual program. I love the fact that I have the freedom to determine my own Higher Guidance in this group. I never have to justify or rationalize my choice, nor do I have to share it with anyone else. No one cares. We have more pressing issues to deal with, like getting our own lives in order. Going to Al-Anon and working through the Twelve Steps helped me find a Higher Guidance that no church or religion ever provided for me. It is stronger than I ever imagined possible.

Another benefit is that meetings are free. They don't replace counseling, but some people find they get as much and sometimes more from the meetings than they do in traditional counseling sessions. Numerous counselors recommend Al-Anon. The only requirement to attend is that you have a loved one with the disease of alcoholism or addiction. I have learned more about living a happy life from Al-Anon than any book, counselor, or church ever taught me, but they all have their place according to what you need.

If you want relief from your misery, heartbreak, fears and from the feeling that something is lacking in your life, attend an Al-Anon meeting. The people there will welcome you with open arms and open hearts. They understand exactly how you feel because they've been there. They don't give advice, but they share what they have done in similar situations, so you come away with many new options for dealing with the disarray in your life.

Participating in the Al-Anon program has been one of the greatest and most life-changing experiences I've ever had. It has helped restore my sanity, my hope, my spirituality, and my worth and improved every relationship I have.

Similarities Between Yoga and Al-Anon—
How They Both Helped Me

Both yoga and the Twelve Steps are spiritual programs, and both involve looking deeply at one's self. I've met people who think yoga is sacrilegious, for it involves worshipping something different than the divinity they're used to. Some people feel that AA/Al-Anon is a cult. Neither is true in my opinion, although I have seen a few cliques in these groups. Both programs help you gather great knowledge about yourself and your worth in the world.

People in these programs find them of value throughout their lives. I could always understand why someone would practice yoga for a lifetime, but I was surprised to learn that some people had been going to Al-Anon for thirty-plus years. At first, I thought that meant they weren't quite getting it or that maybe the program wasn't too effective. I've since realized that the reason people go for so long is because they continue to learn more about themselves and how to apply the principles in every part of life instead of just the addiction part. The philosophy behind both programs is beneficial for dealing with all of life's circumstances. They also help you get to know yourself like nothing I've experienced before.

No one ever told me what or who to worship in either group. In fact, it was by attending Al-Anon and practicing yoga that I felt the freedom to fire my God of old and find a new Higher Guidance.

I have made the most amazing friends in these programs. Both groups have played a huge role in bringing me back home to my natural state; they have helped me find the joy and passion that I had been pushing away as I struggled with my son's addiction. I've seen both programs work miracles in other people's lives as well.

I've witnessed how other philosophies and perspectives can enlarge our viewpoints and awaken something inside us. These are beneficial too. If we're really interested in changing our lives, we have to be open to other perspectives and options; otherwise, we'll end up right where we started. Transformation and change require modifying what we've always done and who we've always been. We must do things differently. We must consider every possible option available to help us on our journey. But only *we* can decide what is beneficial for us.

Trust your instincts to avoid choosing the wrong groups. One mistake you might make is to fall for everything a specific group espouses, losing your own voice and insight in the process. Ask yourself these questions: "If on some issues I believe differently from other people in this group, will I be shunned?" and "Will my voice be silenced in any way?" If the answer to either is yes, it might not be in your best interest to remain a member of the group.

Here's an example. One of the churches I used to attend conducted yearly interviews, a practice I'd never heard of in any other church. Among the questions they asked was this: "Are you associated with any other group that is contrary to what this religion teaches?" I took this to mean any association with pro-abortion causes, gay and lesbian groups, open marriage forums, drinking clubs, and the like. At the time, I could answer no, but I remember thinking that I might someday want to participate in some group or cause of this type. Clearly, what the church was looking for was the kind of blind loyalty that keeps everyone in the same boat, going the same direction on the same body of water, under the same sky… you get the picture. There's not much room for individual freedom or independent thought in a church or other group where you're told how you should believe and act. Feel free to bail from this kind of group mentality if you're uncomfortable with it. Such a group will not support you on your journey if your path takes you in a different direction.

Supporting Others

Many, many good community causes help to make the world a better place. In fact, it can be downright overwhelming to pick the one(s) you want to become involved with.

Perhaps that's as far as you've gone—thinking about your choice. Given your other commitments, you may not have the time or energy to research all these groups, finding out exactly what they do, which ones use their money most judiciously, and how they could take advantage of your specific skills.

So you end up doing nothing, or you choose a cause that sounds reasonable and donate some money, particularly if you need the tax write-off. It is far easier to throw money at a problem than to actually become involved and get your hands dirty. If giving money is the only thing and the best thing you can do, that is okay too. Great causes all need financial resources. For many people, however, that's the easy way out.

In the past, I wasn't much of a volunteer. I thought my spare time was better spent on, well, me. It was easy to ignore important issues or causes because most of them didn't affect me directly. I could turn away and act as if they didn't exist because in my world, they really didn't. I was okay and in a comfortable place, and therefore, I excused myself from helping out.

Once you discover your worth and begin to free up some time (see the discussion in chapter 6), you may be far less inclined to spend your time and energy on doing things to validate yourself; you don't need to anymore. You know you have something valuable and worthwhile to offer the world, and now you have more time to do that. *When you finally realize your own significance, you see others differently; you can't help but realize their significance also—knowing they have the same worth as you.* This knowledge changes everything. You make the shift from building up your self-esteem to sharing your gifts with others so they can discover and dance in their own brilliance too.

Serving others doesn't necessarily require large chunks of your time. If you haven't yet found a worthwhile cause or if you really don't have the time, there are many simple ways to serve others:

1. **Open the door for someone.** Do this even if they're not right behind you and you must wait an extra ten seconds for them to get to the door. Losing a few seconds will not affect your life in any way. Yet the person you help in this manner is usually very grateful that you took the time to do something nice for them, and you'll feel good about doing it. It's such an easy way to let someone know they matter.

2. **Share something you love.** I like to bake desserts and take them to my neighbors and friends. When I was younger, I never thought of it as service. I just loved to make desserts so I could eat them—sharing them was the icing on the cake, so to speak. Now, my reasoning has changed. I bake goodies because I know how happy it makes the recipients to receive these small gifts. The fact that I get to eat some as well is the icing on the cake these days. Most of us love to get something homemade because it's rare that people have time to spend in the kitchen anymore. Sharing treats you've made yourself is definitely a way of serving others that always results in a smile.

3. **Look people in the eye and be the first to say "hi."** Most people will respond when you do these simple things. I used to be very shy, so this was hard for me. It wasn't until I went to college that I learned I needed to do this kind of thing. One of my classmates needed a ride home. Although I didn't know her well, I offered to take her. It turned out that she lived about twenty-five miles out of town, so we had a chance to talk on the way. When I dropped her off, she said to me, "You're not at all like I thought you'd be. I thought you'd be really stuck up when I first saw you, but you're not that way at all. You're really nice." It wasn't the first time I would hear this message, so it eventually dawned on me that it might be beneficial for me to make the first move with others. The experience taught me that people judge quickly and often wrongly. My shyness was perceived as standoffish. By saying "hi" first, you show that you recognize and acknowledge another's presence and worth, whether it's someone you know well or a passing stranger on the street.

4. **Support one another's creative efforts.** If you listen to an entertainer or see a painter on the street or at a coffee shop, drop some money in their jar or guitar case. It takes great courage to put one's work out for public display. Reward their courage and support their efforts to pursue a journey they love. They are sharing their gifts and talents with you.

5. **Make thoughtful gestures.** Shovel off part of the neighbor's sidewalk, mow a section of their grass, and pick up their newspapers if they're out of town. Surprise a coworker with a treat on their desk, buy coffee for the next person in line at your regular coffeehouse, or put a note on someone's pillow or car window that they'll find later. Any little gesture you make lets them know that someone cares about them.

When you give of your time and energy, even if your commitment is small, you create a personal link. It is this human connection that helps us heal and brings us closer to one another. A nicer car doesn't heal, fancy clothes don't heal, and neither do any of the other toys we accumulate. It's not that you can't have those things or that they don't bring a smile to your face, but they can't match the love and care that comes from your fellow man or woman. Acknowledging another's divinity and worth, now that has power!

When Should You Hold Back?

Are there times when you should limit your expression with others? Perhaps. Your actions speak very loudly. Consider this: are you expressing yourself in a way that is either neutral or inclusive of others, or are you behaving in a way that is divisive? For example, I recently saw this bumper sticker: "I'm too informed to vote (fill in the blank)." The point here is that whatever is put in the blank space will cause some people to agree and others to get angry. We all are fortunate to have the right of free speech and the liberty to express personal opinions, but this type of judgmental statement can be harmful, creating separation between our neighbor and us. Can you be more mindful when expressing your viewpoints? Can you bridge the gap with useful or nonconfrontational information instead? Can you accept others' right to their opinions without shoving yours down their throat? You won't stop everyone from indulging in this type of behavior, but you can refuse to participate in it yourself. Remember that you are an example to others and especially to the younger generation.

8

Protective Boundaries: Dealing with Difficult People

The Bullies in Your Life

Standing up to a difficult and hostile person can be extremely hard to do, especially if, at some level, you fear the individual. This kind of fear may impede you in several ways. If it robs you of the power to confront the bully, your voice will be suppressed and your needs will go unmet. And if it keeps you from acting, it may prevent you from bringing positive—and necessary—changes to your life. Outsiders might not perceive the tensions in your relationship with a bully, so you might find that others have trouble understanding why you find making changes so difficult. You, however, know all too well how hard it is to move forward, let alone live with purpose, if you've felt diminished, unloved, and unwanted because of the way another has treated you, particularly if that person is a loved one.

The fear that comes with confronting a bully can be debilitating. If you've ever been in the situation—your heart racing, your breathing fast and labored, your throat constricted, and your stomach pitching—you know exactly what I mean. In the midst of this confrontation, your mind goes blank. You can't remember details to substantiate your own argument or refute the accusations that are being hurled at you. Your voice is silenced as you're dismissed as crazy or stupid, charges you've heard on past occasions when you dared to speak out. Your body tightens up as you try to deflect the verbal barrage. If only you could turn into a compact little ball and just roll away and hide.

Alcoholics, addicts, and dry drunks (who behave like active alcoholics but aren't drinking) can be extremely abusive and manipulative bullies. If you've been on the receiving end of their abuse for any length of time, you begin protecting yourself in the only way you know—by remaining silent and not rocking the boat. You accept unreasonable behavior because of your underlying fear. You may believe there is no way to get out of your situation, and if your sense of your own worth is at rock bottom, you might feel it's not even worth trying.

What Are You So Afraid Of?

What you fear most is that the bully's anger and rejection will be directed at you. A bully can rip you apart with words as sharp as shrapnel. You are terrified of their reaction if you say or do anything contradictory or provocative—and you never know what or when that might be.

Often, your fear of the bully's reaction to any change you might initiate surpasses your fear of change. You know they'll be furious with you if you try to alter anything that directly affects them because they don't want to change. They like things just as they are.

Bullies are experts at intimidation. They can control the direction of a simple conversation and deftly turn it into an argument; they can confuse the facts and twist them around for their own benefit with great ease. When you do speak up, they often seize on something in what you've said and sling it back at you in a totally distorted manner. Somehow, you end up feeling guilty, which only reinforces your instinct to remain silent. You may even feel stupid for standing up for yourself and your needs or trying to contribute anything meaningful to the situation.

How much easier it is to just toe the party line and agree with the bully. Feeling like you are on the same team with them as they express their rage toward another seems preferable to having their rage directed at you.

Complicating things further, you feel a certain amount of love and loyalty toward them, especially if they're a spouse, a child, or another family member. It may be hard to imagine how you could live without them. It takes great courage to change the unhealthy dynamic underpinning your relationship with a bully. But the situation will persist until *you* make the decision to change it.

·{ MY STORY }·

After my divorce and in my children's teenage years, my sons, with the support of their father, felt they had the right to treat me terribly, something they'd never done in the past. I knew they were confused and angry, and in a way, I believed I deserved to bear the brunt of their sadness and uncertainty to a degree. After all, I had caused some of their pain by deciding to divorce their dad.

As a result, I felt awkward and out of sorts, not knowing how to parent them for fear I would make the situation worse. I accepted unacceptable treatment from my sons, just so I could spend time with them. I let them walk all over me, crushing my spirit with their words and actions.

Looking back, I realize that I was the one who had placed myself in a position to be hurt. Instead of blaming my children or their father for their poor behavior, I needed to take responsibility for my own actions. I had to quit playing the victim and stop being a doormat. I needed to pick myself up off the floor and behave differently from then on. In addition, I needed to look at the attachment I had to the role of being "Mom." I could still be my sons' mother, but I didn't have to base my self-worth solely on that identity—or on their behavior. (See Appendix B for "I'd Rather Take a Hit.")

Placing boundaries around bullying behavior is both hard to do and scary. So is removing yourself from the situation. Many times, you have to start with baby steps. One of the initial steps I took involved applying the "reasonable person" test.

The Reasonable Person Test

Back in my college days, I was taught about the reasonable person test. I describe it as the behavior an ordinary, prudent person takes that is both appropriate and reasonable under similar circumstances.

I use this tool when I'm unsure of what to do. I first applied it when parenting my children during the divorce. Since I personally felt out of balance, I asked myself, "What would a reasonable parent do in this situation?" Strangely enough, I found there was a wiser part of me that still knew what was reasonable even though my immediate frame of mind was wild and uncertain. Reframing the question helped me to see things from a better perspective and act accordingly until I got my bearings. I came to understand that, though I could continue letting my sons know that I loved them and that I'd be available for them, I had to accept the situation as it was and let them go, as counterintuitive as that seemed. When push came to shove, I really had no other choice. It was time for me to stop fighting everyone and everything. Clearly, that approach wasn't working. It was only making matters worse.

I began to notice that I actually experienced a measure of peace during those times when my sons wouldn't communicate with me; at least in those moments, there was no fighting or justifying my views.

There was less disharmony as well, and the constant tension we all lived with decreased because my sons weren't placed in the middle.

I knew that the best thing I could do was to get healthy. I was forced to learn how to live without defining myself solely on my role as a mother. If I figured out how to create my own happiness, I thought, perhaps I could set a positive example for my boys, and with any luck, they might notice. That was the best and most sensible option I had left. *Reasonable,* one might say.

You Can't Win at Their Game: The Temptation to Play

Unreasonable people are just that—unreasonable. That simple fact is sometimes forgotten as you begin to get stronger in your own voice. It is often tempting to fight back with your newfound sense of power. I learned this does not work well.

When I did gather the courage to say something, I'd often say it in an inflammatory way. I swung from one end of the spectrum to the other— from not speaking at all to speaking with anger, criticism, and judgment. My voice had no balance, it tottered one way and the other like a child learning to walk.

Oh, sure, on a couple of occasions I might have gotten a few really good digs in or said something amazing that they didn't have a comeback for. But this never ended up being a good long-term strategy for me, and here is why.

If you're not a bully, you don't think like one. You aren't nearly as good at bullying as they are. It took me a while to learn this one, but I had to concede that I would usually come out on the losing end of these battles because of that simple fact. Part of learning to use the power of your voice is knowing when it's best to use it sparingly, cut the conflict short, and minimize the damage.

When you get tired of being a doormat, you pick yourself up and shake yourself off. You gather every ounce of courage you have to pull yourself together, and with great fortitude, you venture into the unknown. The timing is different for everyone. When you decide it is time, it's time.

Setting Healthy and Useful Boundaries

You set boundaries as a way of protecting your peace and serenity from inappropriate or harmful behavior, whether on the part of yourself or others. These barriers are not necessarily erected as a means of keeping others out. (Of course, some distance may be necessary in specific circumstances in order to limit your exposure to hurtful or toxic behavior.)

Many people, especially addicts, have boundary issues. They'll take everything they can from you; encroach upon your private time and space; ignore previously established rules; and rob you of your peace and serenity as often as they can, if you allow it.

Setting boundaries is one of the hardest things to do when you love an addict. Among other things, you worry that they'll think you're withholding your love and support from them. And the guilt just keeps piling up.

When you love an addict, *you* tend to suffer from boundary problems as well. Your obsession with helping them get well causes you to try to handle business that is not your concern.

It's only when you realize just how miserable you've become, coupled with the fact that your addict isn't getting any better (or may be getting worse), that you decide to do something about it. You've hit your own bottom waiting for them to hit theirs.

Setting boundaries and enabling behavior are two sides of the same coin. If you're unable to set an appropriate boundary, you're enabling the other party to take advantage of you. This enabling often causes you to blame them, quite inappropriately, for your own misery. At some point, you'll realize that you have placed yourself in a position to be harmed. Only you can change that situation.

Setting boundaries is another area where baby steps work well. Typically, your mind is so confused and conflicted that you don't have any idea of what boundaries to put into place. Don't fret. You don't need to have all your boundaries figured out at once. Talking with a trusted confidant can help you determine some options that feel right for your specific situation. It is helpful to choose something very small as your starting point, and then you can go from there.

Setting boundaries is one of the hardest things to do when you love an addict.

Your loved one may readily accept the boundary you set, or they might fight it like crazy. So you must be prepared to implement a consequence if and when the boundary is breached. They'll test you over and over to see if you mean what you say. Setting a boundary and not being able to follow through with any consequences is ineffective. Don't do it.

The whole process can be frightening when you begin. Setting boundaries is a new behavior for you, and you'll be afraid of your addict's reaction. But after you place a boundary and it works, you'll be far more empowered—and all the more likely to uphold it again.

There are many types of boundaries. Here are examples of some healthy and useful ones that can make a big difference to your peace of mind:

- **Avoid being at your addict's beck and call.** Don't drop everything in order to answer their phone calls or respond to their emails immediately. Give them the opportunity to work things out themselves, and give yourself some peace in the meantime. You can respond later if necessary.
- **Turn off or mute your cell phone at night.** The goal is to avoid unnecessary disturbances. You might let your loved one know that you'll be doing this.
- **Let them handle their own life.** Allow them to deal with doctor appointments, detox or rehab admissions, insurance issues, court dates and legal issues, paying bills, and arranging for bail money. They are much more capable than you give them credit for. Let their issues be theirs, not yours.
- **Limit access.** Change the code on your garage door, and don't provide a key to your addict if you don't want them in your house. Make sure they call before dropping by unannounced. In this way, your home will be a safe haven for you, plus you'll no longer have to worry that they'll plunder your valuables or come over in the middle of the night.
- **Don't put your life on hold.** If your loved one is late or doesn't show up for an event, proceed with your plans anyway. Order at a restaurant, start eating your meal at home, begin watching the movie, and so on. Have backup plans in place so that instead of feeling mistreated, you'll still be able to enjoy something uplifting.

Disarming Language—Reducing Conflict

If you're finding that the ways you've approached challenging situations with your loved one aren't working, here are some alternate strategies to try. These strategies are simple yet effective, and they allow for dialogue that makes a point without sparking conflict or causing excess harm to either party.

1. **When your feelings get hurt, ask the other person, "Are you intending to hurt my feelings right now?"** Sometimes, they really aren't trying to harm you. This question helps them to realize how you feel without necessarily placing blame on them or causing them to get defensive. It also avoids wrong assumptions on your part.

2. **Use "I need" statements.** For example, say, "I need you to call prior to dropping by" or "I need you to take over paying for your own cell phone." These statements eliminate anger or judgment; they simply state what you need instead of dancing around all the reasons why the addict's behavior is wrong. They may not always like what you say, but it's harder to argue with a direct and honest statement or request; no justification is needed on your part. "I need" statements are also helpful when determining boundaries. They get at the root of your problem—what you need in order to reduce or stop your suffering. Saying you need them to stop using drugs or alcohol will not work, however, unless you're willing to remove your loved one from your life until they oblige.

3. **Don't do for others what they can do for themselves.** Otherwise, you are enabling your loved one. Helping when help isn't needed harms you by stealing your time, energy, and resources. It harms the other person by taking away their responsibility for the decisions that shape how their life turns out. This statement is a good one to keep in mind: "I'll help you as long as you're helping yourself." I used this statement when my son was in active addiction and wanted my help. I found I didn't feel guilty about not helping him if he wasn't doing at least as much for himself.

4. **Give your loved one the dignity to live their life and to fail or succeed on their own.** Each of us is responsible for our life—and only our life. One of my favorite things to say is, "That's why they call it Cyndee's life—I get to make those decisions" (the ones that affect me). It also works when you insert another person's name: "That's why they call it Johnny's life—he gets to make those decisions." It's a great reminder of who should have control over the decisions in their life.

5. **The hula hoop analogy.** This strategy reminds you of what is your business and what isn't. Imagine you have a hula hoop around your body. Your job is to not let anyone get inside your hula hoop (and

thereby take away your choices); it is an imaginary boundary meant to maintain your own personal space. Then, imagine everyone else has a hula hoop around them too. It's your job to stay out of their hula hoops—that is, to keep from intruding on their personal space or choices. Some people actually explain this principle to their loved ones so that if there's any encroachment by either party, it's easy to say, "You're in my hula hoop"; they'll know what that means, no explanation needed. Ask yourself, "Is this my issue?" If not, let it go. Before giving advice or offering a solution, consider questions such as, "Did they ask my opinion? Did they ask for my help?" If not, *there is no need to speak up or give an opinion.* Pausing to ask yourself these questions will help you to avoid a lot of heartache and frustration by detaching yourself from problems that aren't yours to solve.

Maintaining boundaries and altering how you speak to your loved one—or anyone else—go a long way toward establishing and encouraging mutually beneficial relationships and productive conversations. You take control of what you can change: your behavior. You disrupt the past pattern of tired and unproductive behaviors by changing your approach and reaction. You take responsibility for your own peace of mind from here on out.

9

Everyday Wisdom

A Three-Rule Approach for Crisis Survival

Naturally, some situations are more troublesome than others. There will be times when you feel paralyzed by fear or worry. You won't know what to do; your contentment is compromised. Everything seems to be happening so quickly that you can barely breathe.

If you find yourself overwhelmed by a crisis, with your life becoming unmanageable and filled with frenzy, here are three things to focus on each day. They will simplify your life and help you through the current crisis:

1. Connect with your Higher Guidance—especially through meditation.
2. Do whatever your job is that day to the best of your ability—no more, no less.
3. Love (be kind to) all those you come into contact with.

These three rules are extremely effective. They might even be your focus for every day of the year, but they're especially helpful during challenging times. Three things, that's all!

When You're Miserable

I'd like to share this powerful insight: *when you're disturbed, it's often because of you.* This simple statement reminds you that your own thinking can sometimes get in your way. Looking at your behavior can help you understand yourself and pull you out of many upsetting emotional dilemmas. It can enable you to preserve your core of contentment by viewing your situation from a different perspective. Consider these ten questions:

1. **What are you most afraid of?** Usually, this is what you're afraid to lose.
2. **Is your fear true right now, or is it really a false expectation that appears real?**
3. **Is your dilemma a crisis or a situation?** Situations often pass without the need to turn them into crises.
4. **Are you blaming others for your circumstances and therefore putting yourself in the victim role?**
5. **Have you placed yourself in a position to be hurt?**
6. **Have you accepted the current situation, or are you using your self-will to try to change it?** Are you trying to control the uncontrollable?

7. **Do you need to apologize for your behavior or to rectify the situation?** Have you been selfish, manipulative, or dishonest?

8. **In what or whom are you placing your trust? Is it your Higher Guidance?** Or have you decided to control things yourself by reverting to the God of your own reasoning?

9. **Have you forgotten that what other people say or think about you is not a reflection of your worth and none of your business in any case?**

10. **Have you forgotten that another's reaction or behavior is usually not about you at all?** They are most likely reacting based on their own fears and misperceptions. Even though you might feel like you're the recipient of their poor choices or bad behavior, it still is likely to have nothing to do with you.

Whenever you're upset or feeling unbalanced, consider these questions to uncover the source of your distress. What you typically discover is that your behavior is based on fear. What are you attached to and clinging to so tightly? What are you refusing to accept? What are you afraid of losing? Where are you being selfish, manipulative, or dishonest? Are you looking outside yourself to compensate for the feared loss? Can you reclaim your power and shift your perspective instead?

... when you're disturbed, it's often because of you.

Shifting Your Perspective

One definition for insanity describes it as "a lack of perspective and a lack of proportion" (source unknown). Sometimes, all it takes is a shift in perspective to see things differently; then suddenly, what you originally thought loses its power. Your outlook changes.

People often get stuck when they look at a perceived problem through one lens, not realizing its distortion. There's almost always more than one way to view a problem or circumstance. Here are a few personal examples showing how a difference in perspective can alter your present thoughts and beliefs:

- One day when my sons were small, we were having lunch at a restaurant. Our waiter was a young man with a tattoo on his arm. (This was way before tattoos became so popular.) I said to my sons, in an embarrassingly judgmental tone, "Did you see that tattoo on his arm?" as if it was a bad thing. Something possessed me to ask the waiter about it when he brought our food. He told us it was in remembrance of his brother, who'd died. Well, I really felt terrible. The incident has been a lesson to me ever since, reminding me that I don't know what's going on behind the scenes or why people do the things they do. To this day, one of my favorite things to do is to ask people about their tattoos. They almost always have a fascinating story to share that gives me great insight into them as individuals. One of my favorites was a grocery store cashier who told me she had a tattoo in honor of her mother. It was an image of the Earth; in the center was her mother's beautiful face, blending into the globe. It was symbolic for her—Mother Earth.

- Following my divorce, I really struggled with not having my sons with me more of the time. Their absence put a damper on almost everything I did. One particular friend witnessed many of my tears and puffy eyes and sensed my overall sadness. Not long after, my former spouse passed away suddenly after suffering a heart attack. This same friend later mentioned something that really struck me and took me by surprise. She said, "I remember when you used to come over to visit and you were always so sad that you didn't get to see your boys more often. Did you ever stop to think that maybe that was the only time they would have left to spend with their dad before he died? Maybe it was the best thing for them to be able to spend that time with him because that was all they would ever get." Her poignant observation totally shifted my perspective. All at once, I was able to see the situation from an entirely different angle.

- On numerous occasions, I couldn't imagine anything but a bad outcome to my son's addiction. The potential penalties awaiting him after his addiction landed him in jail or in some other bad place seemed so severe that I couldn't conceive of him ever regaining any semblance of the good life I had desperately wanted for him. During one of these times, a trusted adviser asked me this question: "How do you know that this consequence isn't exactly what your son needs to turn his life around?" This idea was just what I needed to hear; it allowed hope to replace some of my sadness and fear.

Seeing your life and its problems through a single lens narrows your focus and leaves you with only limited views. You may dislike the current state of affairs or become fearful and project a negative outcome, yet you forget that there are many other ways to look at things—without judgment. Flipping your perspective gives you new insight and reduces the tendency to feed your fear, making that fear smaller and less powerful.

The Teacher in Everything

When you begin to think differently about your challenges, your outlook changes. Whatever your problems are, each one can teach you something—provided you can see it that way. You can turn supposedly hopeless situations around by asking yourself, "What is this situation trying to teach me?" and "What can I learn?"

What you often perceive as an impediment on your path actually is a necessary part of the path— just as it is for your loved one.

In this way, you can look at the problem as a learning opportunity instead of believing it is some kind of bad luck or punishment designed to block your happiness. What you often perceive as an impediment on your path actually is a necessary part of the path—just as it is for your loved one. But the difficulty you face can only teach you what you need to learn if you don't ignore it. Avoiding the problem or going around it will not be effective. At some point, you must learn to deal with it in order to minimize its power; if you don't, that particular obstruction will continue to pop up in your life and keep you stuck.

One issue that continually comes up for me is patience. When I ask myself that first question, "What is this situation trying to teach me," I learn patience is often one of the answers.

Sometimes, you may not find the answer immediately, but it helps to know that you aren't just wasting time, stuck in a holding pattern of suffering. Your pain is pointing you in a different direction, even if you don't understand exactly where that leads. Your personal growth is actually involved in a productive process.

An obstacle can be a precursor to change by creating an opening to do things in a new way. As we've already discussed, it's normal to resist change, at least initially; avoiding change seems an easier option, but the problem doesn't go away. Resistance holds the obstacle in place and keeps you right there with it. In the meantime, all other paths remain uninvestigated.

Accepting Uncertainty and Change

Dealing effectively with uncertainty is a tough challenge. You'd think we might get used to it, since it's such a common part of life. Your mind often tricks you into thinking that you can only relax and enjoy life when it's on your terms—when things are settled and you've concluded that enough has gone your way that you can finally let go and have fun. Ahhh … the illusion of certainty and its relentless pull!

You must transform the way you perceive things in order to deal with life in a better way, a way that brings less suffering for others and yourself. Accepting the current reality, whether you like it or not, is the first step. You cannot fight what is. Accepting the uncertainty that surrounds that reality, however, is where the real work lies. It's also what holds you back the most.

You might think that your loved one's addiction is the problem, for it may be a certainty, but most of your pain comes from the uncertainty surrounding it. The "what ifs" are what drive you crazy.

Think for a while about your current circumstances. What is causing you the most angst—an impending change? An unfavorable outcome? A perceived loss? What do you fear right now that is causing you to resist life? It probably has something to do with uncertainty.

·{MY STORY}·

Even though I would have had less freedom to teach as I wished after my yoga teaching position shifted to a corporate-designed program, I still found it difficult to quit that job and devote all my time to writing this book. It was a great job, and I loved my students.

I felt I had a calling as a writer, but I was also afraid to pursue it. I didn't know if I'd get another yoga-teaching job that I liked as well, or maybe I would never teach again. The loss of something certain really frightened me.

Who was I if I wasn't a yoga teacher? I wasn't an author—yet. The lack of a label for myself was daunting because it added more uncertainty to my life. Even though I knew that labels don't define a person, sometimes having an "occupation tag" attached to you makes it easier to describe yourself to others (again the need for certainty). I agonized over the decision, wanting to keep a foot in both worlds but afraid of making the wrong call even though many things were lining up for the writing opportunity.

Interestingly, I had recently been teaching my students about *svadharma,* a Sanskrit word meaning "following and fulfilling one's personal nature or purpose." When you fail to honor it you go against your nature and thus suffer spiritually. At the time, I didn't think that I would be the one to set the example of what that principle looked like, but curiously enough, we sometimes teach what we need to learn.

With my husband's blessing, I took the leap into uncertainty. I said goodbye to my students, let the fear of what I was leaving behind slip through my hands, and began writing in earnest. Shortly into the writing process, my husband lost his job of twenty years. Suddenly, I was flooded with fear again because of uncertainty about the future and our finances.

Fear is normal. We all experience it. It's how we deal with it that matters most.

I remembered my own counsel surrounding obstacles. What was the universe trying to teach me? I knew I needed to confront my fear, or it would just expand like a balloon. What was I really afraid of—and was that fear warranted?

I increased my meditation, talked with a trusted adviser, and spent more time on self-reflection and self-study. Before long, several things became obvious.

First, I had to trust more in my Higher Guidance than in the God of my own reasoning. To do otherwise results in misguided action driven by fear. The change in plans didn't mean that things would turn out poorly. Heck, they might turn out far better than I could imagine. I had to trust that I would be okay, regardless of the outcome.

Second, I had to remain patient (my old bugaboo) with the unknown. Resisting it was futile. Trying to rush an answer or force an immediate solution was not helpful or even possible.

I learned an awful lot from this experience. The lessons boiled down to deep trust, acceptance of uncertainty, and patience. Once I took these things into account, life got a lot calmer and my peace returned. I continued to write. I used my fear of uncertainty as an opportunity to write about dealing with that very thing—a familiar struggle for those who care about an addicted loved one; it became the fuel for this section. Meanwhile, my husband found a new job, one that would allow him to work remotely, which is something we had wanted for the previous few years.

Making Difficult Decisions

It takes a lot of courage and trust to make a big change. The truth is, though, that even playing it safe is subject to some ambiguity. The illusion of safety doesn't really protect you; it hides you from yourself and prevents you from looking internally for answers. So you take another motivational class, read another self-help book, and add to your arsenal of coping mechanisms hoping that someone or something other than you will create the change you seek.

When you come to a fork in the road, the pain of staying the same has found you. You are willing to say no to something in order to say yes to something else—even if you don't have an inkling about what that is. In the past, trying harder didn't work. Now you're determined to do things differently. You accept the uncertainty of the unknown in order to change.

Making tough decisions can be excruciating, but staying the same is more painful still. I'll share one especially heartbreaking decision I made. My son moved back home after being clean for nine months. We made an agreement with him that he could live under our roof as long as he stayed clean. If he tested positive for drugs, we would ask him to leave immediately.

Sadly, he tested positive for drugs. The decision to kick my son out of the house was one of the hardest things I have ever done. I wasn't certain what he'd do or where he'd go. He had five dollars and a trash bag full of his belongings.

Heartbreaking choices.

I certainly don't advocate that you do what I did unless it feels right for you. I'm happy to report that the situation turned out well for my son. Being thrown out of his family's home was a turning point for him. Today, my son is well. My relationship with him has been restored and even bettered. His eyes glimmer with promise and hope for the future as they once did. He owns a small business, pays his bills and taxes, and saves for the future. He is almost halfway done with college. He has progressed in many ways I would never have imagined. But it could've gone terribly wrong. If faced with a similar situation, you may choose different consequences.

There's hardly ever a perfect solution, and sometimes, it just doesn't matter whether you take the road going left or the one going right. You learn something in either direction.

? ... Are you at a fork in the road? What is causing you so much pain that you're willing to change your past behavior to do something differently today?

Maintaining a Core of Contentment

Contentment comes when you are in a neutral position—you neither like nor dislike any person or situation in your life. *Nothing needs to change in order for you to be okay.* There's no striving; you are satisfied with things as they are. You may prefer that things be different, but the fact that they aren't doesn't change your general mood, outlook on life, or fundamental worth.

When you are content, you create a different and better approach to each day. You remind yourself that you don't need other people to behave a certain way in order for you to be happy. You maintain a core of contentment even in the midst of situations that deeply sadden or worry you.

Maintaining Your Changes

The effort you've made to reclaim your life from your loved one's addiction is a worthy one; now you must ensure that you protect and preserve the gains you've achieved. Some of the changes required at this stage will be relatively easy, and others will prove more difficult and take more time. Regardless, it will require resilience and dedication on your part in order to avoid falling back into old patterns that bring pain and stress and make life unmanageable.

The following guidelines will help you maintain your gains and continue your progress going forward.

1. **Remain steadfast in your effort to purge the old impressions and misinterpretations of yourself.** Continue to explore who you are through observation, experimentation, and direct knowledge; anything that facilitates the dialogue between body, mind, and spirit will assist you in this effort. For example:

   - Study different types of scriptures, revered texts, and other writings to learn what you are drawn to and become aware of other perspectives you never considered before.
   - Commit to an ongoing mindfulness practice of some sort (yoga, tai chi, meditation, creative endeavors, nature walks, and so forth).
   - Create downtime for yourself. Reduce the amount of time the mind spends churning with distractions. Treat yourself well.
   - Pay attention to those times when you feel closer to your Higher Guidance or more divinely inspired. What's different?
   - Experiment with trusting your Higher Guidance and acting on your intuition. Accept more uncertainty. See what happens.
   - Notice areas where you might be blocked or stuck (for example, in using your freedom of expression, sharing your viewpoints, and being totally honest with another).

2. **Live with total devotion to your Higher Guidance.** This transition may prove difficult at first, especially if you've had a history of personal accomplishment. You will be tempted to take back control and manage things as you see fit. You won't realize you have done so until

you contemplate why you are so miserable and your life is chaotic again. When this happens, as it surely will, let go of the control—it's only an illusion. Embrace your Higher Guidance with utmost devotion, continually surrendering your ego to it, on a daily basis and more frequently if necessary. As you do this, peace will come again.

3. **Grant yourself grace.** When you fail to do the right thing—or the best thing—in any situation, it is not the end of the world. Treat yourself gently, with love and tenderness. You will never have all the answers or behave perfectly in every endeavor you undertake. But you can learn from your experiences and try to do things differently the next time. It may take a long time for you to break certain old patterns. Or you may face situations you never could've imagined. Just do the best you can. No one can ask for anything more.

Meditation Practice—A Simple, Powerful Tool

Meditation exists in many forms and varieties. The basic seated form is widely accepted and may be familiar to you. People often incorrectly assume that meditation requires one to sit quietly and release all thoughts. However, that's darn near impossible for most people. So when you practice meditation, don't feel like a failure when your mind is flooded with thoughts: that *will* happen, but you'll learn to slow down those thoughts significantly.

I would suggest starting your meditation practice with at least five minutes per day, building up to a longer session and/or meditating twice a day. Experiment to see what works best for you. Set a timer if you wish. Make it an important part of your day rather than assigning it a low priority on your list and trying to fit it in when you can. In that way, it will be far more effective; you'll soon notice the difference the practice makes in your life.

Here are the steps to follow for basic seated meditation:
- Find a comfortable seated position in a chair or on the floor. If you're on the floor, you may prefer to sit atop a blanket or two.
- Keep your bottom connected to the ground as the top of your head lifts upward; this posture will elongate the spine and make your breathing easier and smoother.
- Place your hands on your legs, palms up or down—your preference.

- Close your eyes.
- Begin breathing in through the nose and exhaling out through the nose. If you forget or get confused and open your mouth, just start again. This type of breathing engages the parasympathetic nervous system, and that has a calming effect. Breathing in this fashion becomes habitual very quickly.
- Listen to the breath as it goes in and out. Think of it as an ocean wave, coming into and then moving away from the shore.
- When a thought enters your mind, simply acknowledge it and then let it go; resume your breathing and listening pattern.

You might want to try an alternative practice as well. Instead of focusing on the sound of your breath, you can use a mantra, such as "so hum." On your inhale, silently say the word "so," and on the exhale, silently say the word "hum." "So hum" means "I am." Try both methods to find out which you prefer.

10

Powerful Insights
and Inspiration

Loving an Addict: The Resulting Gifts

If you've gotten this far in the book, I applaud you! The work you do on yourself will be some of the most enlightening work you'll do in your lifetime. The concept of having your own life, separate from your addict's, may have seemed impossible at the outset. But that life is yours to claim if you want it.

You may never have imagined that a great amount of good could come from something that seems, and often is, so tragic. If your loved one's addiction has caused you to discover pieces of yourself, recapture them, and change your life, then your work has not been in vain. This simple fact remains: no one can live your life better than you do. You deserve to live it well.

Here are some of the benefits you'll reap from the work you do on yourself as you reclaim your life from your loved one's addiction:

1. You come to know and love yourself much more deeply on all levels: spiritually, mentally, and physically—a treasured lifetime gift. The knowledge of your worth becomes the foundation for great comfort and further insight.

2. You begin to understand the ways in which your actions harm your loved one and yourself. You rarely go as far back into the depths of despair that you once knew, and you don't stay there as long.

3. You become far more honest with others and yourself. You no longer fear the truth, even if it isn't pretty. You let go of untruths you've told yourself in the past.

4. You realize you have many more choices and much greater freedom in how you act and react than you ever before considered. You don't feel continually stuck.

5. You don't blame your problems on others. You no longer play the victim. This mindset gives you the power to choose a course of action that is in your best interest instead of remaining powerless because of another's actions.

6. You learn what you can control and you stop wasting your energy on what is beyond your control.

7. You develop empathy and become less judgmental of others in general. Though you have been in terrible positions, that doesn't define you; you are worthy, as are others who are dealing with their specific life tragedies.

8. You find new hope, joy, laughter, and love (instead of constant fear)—emotions you too rarely experienced before.

9. You no longer fight everything. You begin to participate in your own life and affect its direction with much more passion and intent.

10. You trust in something far greater than yourself and allow it to guide your life. Therefore, you experience peace.

Powerful Insights

The following insights come from some of the small but impactful observations interspersed throughout the book.

- If I imagine an outcome/the worst outcome, it probably won't happen because what usually happens is something that I never could have imagined.
- I can be selfish simply by wanting things my way.
- Whenever I'm disturbed, it's because of me.
- That which is most personal is universal.
- What somebody else thinks of me is none of my business.
- Whenever I'm angry, I'm in self-righteousness.
- Courage cannot exist without fear.
- It's not all about me.
- I don't need other people to behave a certain way, or situations to turn out a certain way, in order for me to be okay.
- You didn't cause it, you can't control it, and you can't cure it—but you can complicate it. (From Al-Anon)
- Whenever I place blame on someone or something else, I remain a victim, with no options and no way of changing my situation.
- Expectations are future resentments.
- Sometimes, the best form of action is nonaction.
- Am I behaving out of self-will or from a place of acceptance?
- You can add to someone's happiness, but you can't *be* their happiness.
- Who is in charge, the God of my own reasoning or my Higher Guidance?
- Where are you holding back? If fear of failure is the only reason you're choosing not to act, then it's not a good enough reason.
- Definition of *insanity:* a lack of perspective and a lack of proportion. (Source unknown)
- Hurt people *hurt* people.
- As long as there's life, there's hope. The story is still being written.

Love and Purpose: Concluding Thoughts

When your heart belongs to an addict, it changes and contorts how you love—it affects both the love you have for yourself and the love you have for those around you.

After reading this book, you should have a better idea of your personal worth and presence. You now better understand what it means to love yourself well and to love others in a healthy manner. At long last, you should be on the way to a liberated life that aligns with your natural tendencies and gifts, despite the circumstances that surround you.

Love can temper fear, soften the hard edges of life, and lift you up from the depths of despair. It can expand your life into one filled with meaning, beauty, and purpose. As the saying goes, "Love is simple, love is kind." There are only two things required to utilize its greatest potential:

1. *Loving yourself,* which happens when you realize, without a doubt, that you have something to offer the world.
2. *Loving others,* which you express by sharing yourself (your gifts and talents) with the world.

Achieving them both *may* be your life purpose.

Namaste—*The divine in me recognizes the divine in you.*

Appendix A

The Yoga Sutras of Patanjali
commentary on Sutra 1:4 by Swami Satchidananda
Reprinted with permission of Integral Yoga Media

You seem to have lost your original identity and have identified with your thoughts and body. Suppose I ask you who you are if you don't identify with anything whatsoever. If you say, "I am a man," you have identified yourself with a masculine body. If you say, "I am a professor," you are identifying with the ideas gathered in your brain. If you say, "I am a millionaire," you are identifying with your bank account; if "a mother," with a child; "a husband," with a wife. "I am tall; I am short; I am black or white" shows your identification with the color and shape of the body. But without any identifications, who are you? Have you ever thought about it? When you really understand that, you will see we are all the same. If you detach yourself completely from all the things you have identified yourself with, you realize yourself as the pure "I." In that pure "I" there is no difference between you and me.

This is true not only with human beings but with everything. You call something a dog because it has a dog's body. The spirit in a dog and a human is the same. The same is true even with inanimate objects; there is the same spirit in a stone or a wall. If I use the term "spirit," or "Self," you might hesitate to believe me, but if the physicist says the wall is nothing but energy, you will believe that. So, using the scientist's language, there is nothing but energy everywhere. Even the atom is a form of energy. The same energy appears in different forms to which we also give different names. So the form and name are just different versions of the same energy. And, according to the Yogic scientists like Patanjali—and even many modern scientists—behind the different forms of energy is one unchanging consciousness or spirit or Self.

That is why, if we could calm our minds and get to the basis of all these modifications, we would find the unity among everything. That is the real Yogic life. That does not mean we are indifferent to the changes and become useless to the world. Instead, with this experience of universal unity we function better. We will have happy and harmonious lives. Only then can we love our neighbors as our own Self. Otherwise, how is it possible? If I identify myself with my body, I will also see another person as a body and the two bodies cannot be one—they are always different. If I identify myself with my mind, nobody can have a mind exactly like mine. No two individuals have the same body or mind, even twins. Even to the extent of the half-inch-square thumb we are not the same.

But behind all these differences, in the Self, we never differ. That means behind all these ever-changing phenomena is a never changing One. That One appears to change due to our mental modifications. So, by changing your mind you change everything. If only we could understand this point, we would see that there is nothing wrong outside; it is all in the mind. By correcting our vision we correct things outside. If we can cure our jaundiced eye, nothing will look yellow. But without correcting the jaundice, however much we scrub the outside things, we are not going to make them white or blue or green; they will always be yellow. That's why Yoga is based on self-reformation, self-control and self-adjustment. When this reformation is accomplished we will see a new world, a harmonious and happy world. That's why we should always keep ourselves free from these wrong identifications.

Appendix B

"I'd Rather Take a Hit"

By Marian Camden, Psy.D.

Jane couldn't figure out what was wrong with her. She had a good job, a nice home, great kids, and an attractive, successful husband. Her friends all thought she was lucky to have such a good life. Yet Jane felt depressed, uneasy, confused, unsure of what she really did feel, and very ashamed of her seeming inability to be happy. Her husband Carl told her she had a "hormone problem," that she "took things too seriously," or that maybe she just didn't *want* to be happy.

Strangely, when Jane finally decided to see a therapist, Carl teased her about it—a lot. He didn't like it when she went to appointments and liked it even less when she took the therapist's advice and started spending more time with her friends and doing special activities she enjoyed. Carl thought she was "running away" from her problems and taking her therapist's word too seriously.

It took a long time for Jane to recognize that it was actually Carl who didn't want her to feel happy and confident. He wanted—even needed—her to feel ashamed, confused, and emotionally needy. Carl only laughed at her when she tried to talk with him about what she was seeing. "You've always been a little paranoid, Jane. Remember?" After months of standing up for herself, only for Carl to laugh at, put down, and disempower her over and over again, Jane filed for a divorce. It was scary and difficult, but she knew inside that she was making the right decision—a new and very important feeling for her.

"Quit Making Such a Big Deal about It!"

"You're too sensitive." "I was just kidding." "You're crazy." "I never said that—you remembered it wrong." Those phrases don't sound too terrible, do they? They can't be as hurtful as cursing or yelling, right? Wrong!

Emotional abuse is sneaky, subtle, and pervasive; most people don't recognize it in the moment, even when it has them by the throat. That's part of what makes it so dangerous. Victims of emotional abuse are often in deep trouble before they even realize they are being abused. They are filled with self-doubt, shame, and confusion. It's hard for them to trust their own judgment or even to assert what they know to be true.

So often, victims who have also suffered physical abuse say, "I'd rather take a hit than deal with the emotional abuse again." The pain from a slap or a punch fades away. The shame, confusion, and helplessness that victims of emotional abuse feel can take up residence inside for years and taint everything they think, feel, and do. Because this form of abuse is often so subtle, many victims don't even realize that an outside force has led them to feel so badly about themselves.

"Crazy, Stupid, and Bad"

One good definition of emotional abuse is: an ongoing pattern of interaction with another person in which one person's abilities, perceptions, beliefs, needs, and desires are consistently disregarded or demeaned in the service of putting the other person in a position of false security and power. Emotional abuse is an attack on your fundamental ability to perceive and respond to reality accurately. Jane later described her emotional abuse this way: "It was like Carl would jab a pin in my eye and then tell me I had a problem when I told him it hurt."

Like any other type of abuse, emotional abuse knows no boundaries in terms of social class, education, or income bracket. In fact, the more sophisticated an emotional abuser is, the harder the abuse is to recognize, and, consequently, the more damaging its effects. No matter where the abuse comes from or how it's served up, the outcome is always the same: believing you are crazy, stupid, and bad. The poison in emotional abuse is that it turns innocent victims against themselves.

By the time Jane realized what was happening to her, she had lost faith in her ability to care for her children, to do her job well, or simply just to be a decent and worthy person. How could she be so wrecked inside when Carl never raised his voice, let alone his hand to her? Simply put, he made her crazy. You are "crazy," in terms of emotional abuse, when you do not believe what you see, know, or feel because you are letting someone else's manipulations take charge of your reality. The kind of crazy that comes from emotional abuse makes you believe someone else's destructive words instead of what you know and feel inside yourself.

What Abusers Do and Why

In therapy, Jane's therapist was surprised to hear her describe herself as "selfish," "angry," "resentful," and "jealous." She tried hard to do better, be better, but somehow it always turned out that she had gotten it wrong again, according to Carl. He seemed so kind and supportive when she was feeling down, always pointing out where she had gone wrong in her thinking—except that there was nothing wrong with her thinking. Jane wasn't unusually selfish, angry, resentful, or jealous. Carl was.

A key feature of emotional abuse is the projection of the abuser's negative traits onto the victim. Abusers with anger problems convince their victims that *they* are the ones with anger problems. Abusers who are irresponsible can convince the most conscientious partners that *they* are careless and lazy. Victims of emotional abuse often believe they are "too selfish" when the opposite is more often the case: emotional abuse victims neglect their own needs and feelings.

Like Carl, abusers act in a seemingly kind and supportive manner when they have their victims where they want them: needy, confused, and very, very emotionally dependent. When Jane started to feel good and confident again, Carl somehow found a way to get her back into a place of weakness and dependence. It might have started with something as simple as a comment about her hair or clothing, maybe a remark about the kids needing her attention more. When Jane tried to talk with Carl about his concern, asking questions to try to understand, he would deftly change the subject, say things in ways that undermined her confidence, or correct her "mistaken" perceptions of what he meant, continuing his manipulation until Jane was lost in a mental fog. She felt sure of only two things: that he was right and she was wrong.

Emotional abuse victims are quick to believe the best about others and the worst about themselves. They might be naïve or a bit insecure. Emotional abusers capitalize on these tendencies in order to maintain a sense of superiority and control in the relationship. Emotional abusers need others to be weak and dependent in order to feel OK about themselves and to convince themselves that they won't be abandoned.

Like any other kind of abuser, many emotional abusers don't believe they are worthy of the love of a healthy and independent person, or they have grown up without a chance to learn to trust in a truly equal and sharing relationship. They use belittling, shaming, questioning, and "crazy-making" to tie others to themselves in unhealthy ways. Often, abusers have also been abused and deserve pity more than fear; however, when you are trying to free yourself from the snare of an emotionally abusive relationship, it is important to focus on your own needs first and foremost.

To make things worse, victims of emotional abuse often do not get much support from their family, friends, and community. Often the emotional abuser is a well liked, friendly, charming person. No one but perhaps the victim sees the manipulation, shaming, and constant questioning of his or her reality. Even friends who mean well can tell victims they are "too sensitive" or just need to let it "roll off their backs." With no one to help them recognize the craziness of what they are being fed, abuse victims can get stuck in their false helplessness and hopelessness for a long time.

Reclaiming Your Life

It's not easy to get free from an emotional abuser, and it's harder still to stop abusing yourself emotionally. Changing these patterns can be especially difficult when emotional abuse leads to or takes place during a divorce. It takes a lot of strength to keep believing you have the need and right to live an emotionally safe life and to be treated respectfully when the other party is actively working to make sure you don't get to. Learning or relearning to hear your own thoughts more "loudly" than the thoughts of the abuser takes time and practice.

Self-doubt is the biggest obstacle to overcome and emotional self-reliance is the biggest skill to learn when healing from emotional abuse. It helps to have a therapist, spiritual mentor, friends, or family members who truly believe in you and your ability to trust yourself. During the actual divorce process, it also helps to have an attorney who can recognize emotional manipulation and help you get refocused on reality. In addition, an excellent resource for recognizing and getting free from emotional abuse is Patricia Evans' revealing and practical book, *The Verbally Abusive Relationship: How to Recognize It and How to Respond.*

Here are some things that you can be aware of and do as you free yourself from emotional abuse:

- An important step in getting out of the emotional abuse trap is letting yourself see the damaging behavior for what it really is. That unfunny joke or falsely helpful comment really is meant to put you down, sap your strength, and confuse your thinking. You didn't get it wrong. You aren't "too sensitive." You are seeing reality.
- Be aware that the abuser will give you "change back messages" to try to get you back into that needy, fearful place. An example of such a message is: "Oh, come on, one drink isn't going to hurt," spoken to an alcoholic family member who is working on sobriety. Another might be, "You never had a problem doing all the housework yourself before. Are you PMS-ing or something?" Abuse of any kind can get worse when victims first stand up for themselves, so be prepared. Learn to avoid falling back into the trap.
- The good news about emotional abuse and divorce is that you are taking steps to remove yourself from a harmful force in your life. You don't have to spend the rest of your days believing the worst about yourself. You can set limits and boundaries and decide for yourself what is OK with you and what is not.
- Communicate via e-mail or only through attorneys unless and until the emotional abuser can communicate "just the facts" rather than manipulations and guilt trips.

- If you have children, get healthy for them! A great motivator for lots of moms and dads is not wanting their kids to suffer the same kind of emotional pain they have endured. So, if you want them to be strong inside, to know how to trust themselves rather than the workings of emotional manipulators, *you* should learn how to heal and stay strong.
- Learn to say things like "no," "cut it out," and "you may see it that way but I don't." Memorize a few phrases like these to repeat as often as you need to.
- Doing something physical to end an abusive and unproductive conversation is often necessary. Avoid the "deer in the headlights" trap and *do something* to end the conversation. Say, "I'm hanging up the phone now," and really hang it up. Say, "I'm not willing to be spoken to like this," and walk out of the room, get into your car, or do whatever it takes to show that you are now back in charge of your life—and that the emotional abuser is not.

Emotional abuse is a sneaky, difficult, hard-to-explain kind of problem, but it is very real and serious. Those who suffer from emotional abuse can't always tell you exactly what happened, how, why, when, and in what order, but they can tell you that their lives were diminished and they did not like who and what they had become. The good news is that it's never too late to reclaim your sanity and your life.

Whether you are in an abusive marriage, dealing with an abusive ex, or learning to have a different kind of relationship after a divorce, you always have the right to think your thoughts and feel your feelings without being shamed and manipulated. You might not get the abuser to treat you as you would like to be treated, but you can protect yourself from further abuse, stop "needing" the abuser, and learn to trust, love, and enjoy the healthy, peaceful, respectful place you create within your own mind and heart.

Marian Camden, Psy.D., is a licensed psychologist specializing in divorce-related court evaluations and psychotherapy with children and adults, as well as physical and emotional trauma and abuse recovery. She can be reached at (720) 493-4827.

References and Recommended Readings

Books and Articles

Alcoholics Anonymous. *The Story of How Many Thousands of Men and Women Have Recovered from Alcoholism* (widely known as the "Big Book"). New York: Alcoholics Anonymous World Services, Inc., 1974.

Beattie, Melody. *Codependent No More*. Center City, Minn.: Hazeldon Publishing, 1992.

————. *The Language of Letting Go: Daily Meditations for Codependents*. Center City, Minn.: Hazeldon Publishing, 1990.

Camden, Marian, Psy.D. "I'd Rather Take a Hit." *Divorce in Denver—Moving Forward* 2, no. 4 (July/August 2006): 18–23.

Chodron, Pema. *When Things Fall Apart: Heart Advice for Difficult Times*. Boston: Shambhala Publications, Inc., 1997.

Easwaran, Eknath, trans. *The Bhagavad Gita*. Tomales, Calif.: The Blue Mountain Center of Meditation, 2007.

————. *The Upanishads*. Tomales, Calif.: The Blue Mountain Center of Meditation, 2007.

Evans, Patricia. *The Verbally Abusive Relationship: How to Recognize It and How to Respond*. Avon, Mass.: Adams Media, 2010.

Paramahansa, Yogananda. *Autobiography of a Yogi*. Los Angeles: Self-Realization Fellowship, 1998.

Satchidananda, Sri Swami, trans. *The Yoga Sutras of Patanjali*. Buckingham, Va.: Integral Yoga Publications, 1990.

Spence, Gerry. *Seven Simple Steps to Personal Freedom, An Owner's Manual For Life*. New York: St. Martin's Press, 2001.

Tolle, Eckhart. *A New Earth: Awakening to Your Life's Purpose*. New York: Penguin Books, 2005.

Williamson, Marianne. *A Return to Love*. New York: HarperCollins, 1993.

Online Sources

Al-Anon.org. For those recovering from another's drinking

Nar-Anon.org. For family and friends of an individual with a drug addiction

Theodosiou, Barbara: The Addict's Mom Facebook Group

About the Author

Cyndee Rae Lutz has evolved with her life circumstances, including starting a successful magazine, *Divorce in Denver—Moving Forward,* following her divorce and becoming a yoga teacher as well as a Twelve Steps mentor in Al-Anon after her son became addicted to drugs. In *When Your Heart Belongs to an Addict,* her first book, she combines wisdom from these and other philosophies and spiritual practices with her harrowing yet transformative experience as the mother of an addicted son. The result is a practical set of tools to help others survive and thrive in the shadow of addiction.

As an author, speaker, life coach, and self-described "light-hearted rebel," Cyndee helps people understand their inherent worth and reclaim their lives from societal expectations, codependencies, and the effects of a loved one's addiction or challenging circumstances. She is a compassionate, approachable resource, and her desire to guide individuals toward their better selves drives both her personal and professional endeavors.

In her free time, Cyndee logs miles upon miles in her walking shoes—often accompanied by her standard poodles—and practices yoga and meditation. A lifelong learner, she is open to all she hasn't yet imagined. She lives with her husband in Centennial, Colo.